THE SPECTACLE OF EMPIRE

THE SPECTACLE OF EMPIRE

Style, Effect and the Pax Britannica

JAN MORRIS

faber and faber

London   Boston

First published in 1982
by Faber and Faber Limited
3 Queen Square London WC1N 3AU

British Library Cataloguing
in Publication Data

Morris, Jan
The Spectacle of Empire
1 Commonwealth of Nations – History
I. Title
909′. 0971241081   DA18
ISBN 0–571–11957–3

Designed and produced for Faber and Faber Limited by
Bellew & Higton Publishers Ltd
17–21 Conway Street, London W1P 6JD

Typeset by Phoenix Photosetting, Chatham
Colour separations by Fotographics Ltd
Printed and bound in the United Kingdom by W. S. Cowells

CONTENTS

PROLOGUE

At the end of the nineteenth century the British Empire, the largest empire in history, achieved a kind of fulfilment: not just of political, historical or economic ambition, but of spectacle and of style. A tumultuous century of wars, explorations, emigrations, inventions and distant adventures was given expression in this moment, and the great Empire seemed to stand there like a huge work of art, resplendent and complete.

This was an extraordinary triumph of national character over circumstance. The British Empire had been acquired piecemeal over the generations, spanned every category of climate and terrain, and embraced almost every race and creed imaginable; yet such was the confidence of the British then, so potent was their propaganda and their self-persuasion, that they managed to present the whole immense contraption as an aesthetic unity. For long afterwards, until the dissolution of British power in fact, the subject territories remained clamped in the manners imposed upon them at the end of Queen Victoria's reign; and to this very day, when people think of British imperialism they think more often than not in terms of the modes, displays and behaviours of the imperial *fin-de-siècle*. As the critic Robert Byron wrote in the 1930s, the British Empire created 'a permanent nineteenth century'.

This fully evolved *objet d'histoire* is the subject of this book. It is about the impression the Empire gave – not so much to its subjugated peoples, whose view of it was sometimes very different, as to the rest of the world, and not least to its own creators. The book looks back, in paintings and old photographs, to the events which led to the culmination of the 1890s; it looks forward to the Second Boer War which, only a few years later, dampened the spirit of the great enterprise while solidifying, perhaps, its forms. There has never been a national *persona* more powerful than that of the imperial British at the height of their self-esteem: these pages set out, by using the Empire's own images, to capture a little of its ambiguous allure.

The text is mostly generalization, or more properly impressionism, but at the back of the book there are some geographical and even statistical facts, to bring it down to detail.

Hoisting the Flag: British sovereignty is established at Port Moresby, New Guinea, 1884

CHAPTER ONE

TOP OF THE BILL

Proclaiming Queen Victoria Empress of India, Delhi, 1877

The British Empire was one of history's odder phenomena. Though it sprang from the loins, as it were, of a smallish nation of European islanders, for a generation or two it governed the destinies of the world: at the climax of its power, around the turn of the twentieth century, it ruled a quarter of the earth's land surface, and nearly a quarter of its inhabitants. There had never been anything like it, for it far outstripped not only its contemporary rivals, but also the empires of the ancients.

Ideologically it was a muddle of motives, ideas, myths, pretensions, misconceptions and social attitudes, never unanimous in its intentions, improbably headed by a partnership of the oldest hereditary monarchy and the most venerable parliamentary democracy. It embodied no over-riding principle of purpose. Seen in the clearer light of retrospect, even its loftiest aspirations seem illusory and theatrical, and so hard is it to disentangle its good from its bad, its truth from its deceptions, that most of us remember it less vividly now as a political organism than as a sort of gigantic exhibition.

We have forgotten its statistics, even its extent, but we can see the theatre of it still – the flags and the scarlet uniforms, the grey ships at sea, the imperial railways speeding across their viaducts, the grave palaces of justice and the frontier fortresses, the cities of Empire sleeping in the northern night or astir in southern sunshine, the panache of polo players, the complacency of colonial merchants, the swagger of subalterns, the proud but portly figure of the Queen-Empress herself, Alexandrina Victoria, the impresario or perhaps circus-mistress of this inconceivable performance, stately in statuary from Rangoon to Vancouver, or hemmed about by aides and cavalrymen as she sweeps in her barouche through the streets of her imperial capital.

Spectacle was always an instrument of British imperialism. Queen Victoria's Empire had originated, in the seventeenth and eighteenth centuries, in a very different kind – as a more frankly commercial enterprise, with trading establishments in the east, plantations and settlement colonies in the Americas. But it had depended even then largely upon effrontery: a few bold spirits, infinitely far from home, establishing themselves in unknown parts to sell their goods, grow their crops, build their homes and live their particular lives in the face of all odds. Braggadocio was of the essence in such a venture, and the manner of the Empire in its heyday had its beginnings in those lonely early years, when to show hesitation was to court disaster, and the grander you were, the safer.

Over the years the instinct had deepened, and it had become a maxim of British imperial method that ostentatious effect was not only necessary to survival, but essential to domination too. This was partly, perhaps, the experience of the governing classes at home in Britain. According to one of its most devoted laureates, the poet W. E. Henley, the British Empire was 'an empire of us Anglo-Normans' – an empire, that is, run by the very class which still ran Britain itself (or run at least by its hereditary tenets, for the Scots were great imperialists too). The monarchy which stood at the head of the hierarchy maintained its position with elaborate machineries of ritual and tradition, and the aristocracy at large had long before discovered that splendour worked: as the English saying had it, everybody loved a duke, and the landed classes of England had triumphantly survived the social convulsions that had wracked the rest of Europe. Ensconced in their lovely country houses, surrounded by their acres of park, farmland and deer forest, attended by their deferential tenants, sustained by the treasures they had acquired by war, acumen or skulduggery over so many generations, they prospered there as a very paradigm of imperial dominance. LET CURZON HOLDE, as the motto of one patrician imperialist declared, WHAT CURZON HELDE.

Then to this old instinct of *noblesse*, translated to such different estates abroad, there were added exotic influences picked up in the field. In Africa the native fondness for glitter was interpreted by the imperialists as an inborn susceptibility to swagger – tribal chieftains, after all, maintained their supremacies with prodigious ostentation. The British accordingly adopted similar approaches in their own African enterprises; when in 1890, for instance, they wished to negotiate a distinctly dubious treaty with King Lobengula of the Matabele, they sent as their plenipotentiaries to the King's kraal four well-built officers of the Royal Horse Guards, resplendent in breast-plates, gleaming thigh-boots, clanking swords and plumed helmets.

In India, the cornerstone of the imperial structure in the east, the theory was carried to more majestic lengths. There the indigenous rulers had lived in a style to which Queen Victoria herself was hardly accustomed, the greatest of them maintaining a gorgeous state unparalleled, perhaps, since the excesses of the later Roman emperors. It was the contention of the British that this splendour must be matched, even outshone, if their own suzerainty was to be maintained: whether this was, as they claimed, to overawe the natives, or whether it was really to sustain their own confidence, they certainly put the principle into terrific practice, and governed India always with a show of overweening extravagance (or as Jawaharlal Nehru, one of their most formidable opponents, preferred to put it, 'vulgar ostentation').

By the imperial noonday, then, the spectacle of the empire was flamboyant indeed, coloured as much by oriental despotism and barbaric gesture as by feudal example from nearer home. If it was modernist in some ways, it was antique in others. It embodied the marvellous energy of steam as well as the immemorial pride of horseflesh. It was queenly, but it was savage. It was partly the consequence of dukes, but partly the beat of jungle drums, and imperial activists of every kind were recruited willy-nilly into its presentation: bishops beside viceroys, police officers and railwaymen, even sportsmen, foresters, jute merchants, river pilots or colonial accountants – all of whom, by their bearing, their demeanour or their costume, their pose at the wicket, the flutter of their gowns, the gravity of their presence behind study desk or board-room table, contributed to the imperial effect.

Of course spectacle was not enough. The visual impact of it all had to be supported not just by power, which was implicit to the very existence of empire, but by something in between the two – not merely illusion, not altogether reality – which can best be identified as style. Style was at once the impulse and the product of the imperial performance. Style was how the imperialists converted their own projections into a manner of life and an attitude of mind.

The style of the British in their imperial mood was enormously potent, and was copied and envied everywhere. Lampooned though it would often be in the disillusioned aftermath of empire, we can recognize it now as one of history's great transforming energies. It too was evolved from many sources. Again there was the prevailing social structure in England itself, which made every man, and even more perhaps every woman, feel either superior or inferior to every other, and gave to each grade of society its allotted modes and manners. There was the example of the public schools, forcing grounds of the imperial style, where it was honed and tempered into effectiveness. There was the influence of evangelical Christianity, with its extraordinary combination of arrogance and humility. There was the legacy, however indirectly experienced, of the Industrial Revolution, which gave the British abroad an overwhelming sense of material superiority, as they saw their steamships and locomotives dominating the whole world's trade routes, and found that half humanity's artefacts had been made in Birmingham.

There was the lustre of British national history, too, so constant, so triumphant. There was the very separateness of the British islands, which made the islanders feel superior to their neighbours – VIOLENT STORM IN THE ENGLISH CHANNEL, as the apocryphal *Times* headline was supposed to have said, CONTINENT ISOLATED. There was the pound sterling, much the most powerful of all currencies, which could make and break Powers. There was Shakespeare. There was Nelson. There was Queen Victoria. There was the Sceptred Race itself.

All these influences then, and many more, shaped the attitudes of the British when they left their islands and went out to rule an empire. The product was instantly recognizable anywhere in the world – nineteenth-century observers of many nationalities concur in saying that the Englishman abroad was unmistakable. Nor were the effects merely sub-conscious; often the imperialists deliberately acted them out – sometimes *over*-acted them. Alexander Kinglake the writer recorded such a charade as early as 1835. He was crossing the Sinai desert, alone but for his Greek servant and his Bedouin guides, when he met an Englishman similarly attended coming in the opposite direction, on his way home from India. They took not the slightest notice of one another, so powerful were the conventions that governed their behaviour, but passed each other silently on their camels, there in the heart of the illimitable desert: and it was only when their servants stopped to talk that the two Englishmen allowed themselves to do the natural thing, and exchange the greetings of travellers and fellow-countrymen.

Such was the idiosyncratic style of the Pax Britannica, the Peace of the British which really did give the world some measure of security throughout

Queen Victoria's reign. For all its theatricals there was nobility to it: not just the nobility of courage, which was never in short supply, but the nobility of sacrifice too, among people who truly thought they were, by going out to those distant and demanding fields of enterprise, doing the world a service. There was a fine stoicism: the stiff upper lip might have been stiffened by the egregious cold baths and beatings of the public schools, but it was not without honour (or humour) in the end. That desert reticence – 'I don't think we've been introduced' – certainly looked silly sometimes, but it also reflected a decent respect for privacy, and a reluctance to gush. The well-known British habit of dressing for dinner in improbable circumstances, while it provided material for a whole generation of cartoonists and comedians, nevertheless did represent a brave resolve to keep one's self-respect. 'Fair play' might seem a hypocritical ideal, on the lips of a conqueror, but throughout the Victorian era, all the same, the Englishman's word really was generally regarded as his bond.

But with the admirable there came the rotten. The style of this imperium was partly plain snobbery, and partly racialism, and partly *hubris*, and partly conceit. The self-consciousness of the imperialists, which made for a seemly unobtrusiveness in some situations, made for poses, shams and frauds in others. The ethos of the White Man's Burden shaded easily enough into prejudice. So resolutely British were the British then, so sure of their God-given right to rule the world, that a miserable gulf arose almost everywhere between rulers and ruled, bridged only as often as not by class (everybody loved a maharajah), machismo ('You're a better man than I am, Gunga Din'), sycophancy and occasionally sex.

Except in war, when the British could be extremely brutal, violence was seldom a tool of imperial policy, but hardly less hurtful to the subject peoples was an attitude which lay at the very heart of this style, and underscored all its habits: the attitude of aloofness, which gave the British psychological or even technical advantages indeed, but which denied them the power of empathy, and was their greatest cruelty really.

For many years these postures succeeded, and seen as an aesthetic construction by the last decades of the nineteenth century the British Empire was complete. It had reached its apogee as a political force, and its fruition as theatre too. A fierce intensity of imperial action and feeling had fused the impression permanently, as a potter fires his clay: for between the 1870s and the 1900s everything seemed to happen at once to the British Empire – a plethora of champions arose to glory, battles were fought all over the world, enormous new territories were acquired, roads and railroads were audaciously built, great explorations were concluded, unforgettable pro-consuls blazed across that stage, troops of artists hymned the imperial mission, politicians shamelessly exploited it, and the whole nation seemed seized or even possessed by the craze. The style was frozen there and then: the act reached the top of the bill.

In 1900 there were only some 41 million citizens of the United Kingdom: yet by the exertion of their corporate personality they ruled an alien population of some 340 million souls. Hardly anybody, rulers or ruled, then thought this wicked. The British generally thought it exceedingly virtuous, the subject peoples took it as an Act of God. The Empire seemed immovable, inevitable, winning all its battles in the end, appearing to have no serious rivals, and bearing itself with the serenity of absolute assurance. It was half pretence in fact, for Britain was not so powerful as it appeared, and was fast being overtaken by new industrial rivals, but the spectacle and the style made it all seem feasible – the spectacle, by suggesting that strength untold, riches uncountable, lay behind the façade of empire, the style, by making the British always seem a more formidable people, a more *different* people, than they really were.

Very soon, with the humiliations of the Boer War in the first years of the twentieth century, the confidence would begin to crack, the pace to falter, but by then the British Empire had made of itself an idiom never to be expunged – 'a permanent nineteenth century'. It had cast its unmistakable effect around the whole world, feared and respected, loved and loathed, and properly represented by the rich splodges of red which, in the then popular Mercator projections, lay across the five continents like spilled claret, or shed blood.

Celebrating the Diamond Jubilee of Queen Victoria, Kandy, Ceylon, 1897

The Coronation Durbar, Delhi, 1903: above, the Viceroy, Lord Curzon, with Lady Curzon in the viceregal howdah; left, the grand procession of the elephants past the Red Fort

Scenes of ceremonial life: the Coronation Durbar, Delhi, 1903

Scenes of domestic life: an Indian tea-party,
an Indian butler, an Indian dhobi, and croquet on the lawn at
Canterbury, New Zealand, in the 1860s

Boats of Empire: top, the British Commissioner's Boat, Moorsha Bagh, Kashmir, *c.* 1890;
above, Captain W. Watts's steam-launch *Ruth*, decorated for the visit of Lord Aberdare, lately
Lord President of the Council, to Vancouver in 1890

'Celebrating the Proclamation of Queen Victoria as Empress of India' M. E. Caddy, 1877

'Ball on Board HMS *Galatea* at Calcutta' N. Chevalier, 1870

'Queen Victoria Outside St Paul's Cathedral, Jubilee, 1897' John Charlton

'Royal and Viceregal Party Witnessing the Procession of Native Chiefs Outside the Mori Gate'
(during the Delhi Durbar) Sheldon Williams, 1903

'An Incident During the Tour of HMS *Bacchante*, Barbados' anon, 1879

Preparing for the Shoot

52.B.

"Vigilant", self & crew at Ihota point, after the
circumnavigation of Lake Bangweulu. —

Mr P. Weatherby and the crew of the launch *Vigilant*, after the circumnavigation
of Lake Bangweulu, Northern Rhodesia, *c.* 1900

Preparing for the Camel Ride

Scenes of imperial tourism: Britons crowd the verandah of
Shepheard's Hotel, Cairo, in the 1880s, while other imperialists
cope with the Cairo bootblacks and inspect souvenirs on
the verandah of Watson's Hotel, Bombay

Scenes of imperial tourism: Lady Elgin, Vicereine of India, rides in her palanquin, *c.* 1895, and lesser activists are conveyed by rickshaw in Cape Colony, by carrying chair in the Indian Himalayas, and by piggy-back in Somaliland, *c.* 1890

On the plantation: above, sugar planters and coolie children, Trinidad, 1893; left, coolies on a Ceylonese estate, *c.* 1880

Zululand, 1894: Mr Maxwell, Magistrate in the Umfolozi district (top)
awaits the payment of hut tax from the assembled chiefs (above)

Convicts on the treadmill, India, *c.* 1880

CHAPTER TWO

FAR-FLUNG

Shipping on the Suez Canal, *c.* 1880

In 1894 Rudyard Kipling, writing about the distant expanses of the British settlement empire, coined the word 'far-flung' (*the far-flung, fenceless prairie/Where the quick cloud-shadows trail . . .*). It caught on famously, for it exactly fitted the temper of the imperial times. It was obscurely biblical in tone, hinting at the providential nature of British dominion, and it seemed to possess in its very syllables some essence of the Empire's vastness and variety.

For if the whole Empire was clamped within the spectacle of Britishness, part of that spectacle was its own diversity. The British themselves might be recognizable everywhere, but they certainly imposed no uniformity upon the 11 million square miles of their subject territories. How could they? To a degree unexampled among the empires of history, Queen Victoria's dominions embraced examples of almost every climactic, geological, geographical, ethnic, religious, social, architectural, industrial and cultural kind. Every degree of human progress was represented somewhere in that red on the map, and the subjects of the Queen, at the end of the nineteenth century, ranged from the most exquisite exemplars of the European tradition to elemental aborigines of swamp or wilderness.

The Empire contained, in Australia, Canada, New Zealand and South Africa, several complete modern nations. It contained an entire civilization in the sub-continent of India. It contained Crown Colonies, from Fiji to Bermuda, in all stages of political sophistication. Isolated strongpoints all over the world, huge slabs of Africa like Kenya or Nigeria, famous islands or rocks nobody had ever heard of, archipelagos like the balmy Leewards or the howling Falklands, rich territories of the east like Burma and Malaya – all these made up the vast mosaic, each a chip of different nature, size, value, condition and temperament. Though in theory Parliament at Westminster remained the supreme authority for them all, with the Queen as universal suzerain, and though every imperial citizen was supposed to enjoy equal rights, still a hardly less spectacular diversity of administrations had been devised, over the years, to cope with the profusion of it all: if New Zealand was a parliamentary democracy at least as advanced as Britain itself, India was an autocracy with no public participation in government at all, Ireland was officially part of the United Kingdom, Egypt was ostensibly subject to the Sultan of Turkey, Sarawak had its own White Rajah, Rhodesia was run by the British South Africa Company and Tristan da Cunha enjoyed no government whatever.

One element made a unity of them: the sea. This was a maritime Empire, and to get a panoramic glimpse of the whole of it, to understand something of what 'far-flung' really meant, we must follow the sea-routes.

Of these the most famous, important and allegorical was the Suez Canal in Egypt, so central to the pattern that it had earned itself another favourite imperial cognomen, 'The Lifeline of Empire'.

You could best grasp the symbolic flavour of this waterway by approaching it from the land, for then the canal itself was invisible in the dun expanse of the desert, and all seemed wonderfully stage-managed for effect. The eastern sun, that prerequisite of far-flungness, beat splendidly down upon the scene. The dry wind whistled faintly on the air, and raised sudden sand-eddies in the heat. And presently from somewhere in the north there would sound the insistent thump of reciprocating engines, and one saw advancing steadily through the waste the masts, funnels and upperworks of the south-bound Suez convoy. The ships' hulls did not show, but that only added to the tremendous suggestiveness of the picture, and gave it a sense of ordained and inexorable movement.

Now was the time to run to the canal-edge and climb the levée: for then one discovered with a thrill of pride, as the vessels came slowly by, that they were British almost every one – from stern after stern there hung, limp in the heat but brightly-laundered, the 'Red Duster' so dear to the imperial yarn-spinners and propagandists. What a mighty distribution of power, wealth and purpose that passage of the flags implied! Here was a stocky Liverpool freighter, say, rusty perhaps but workmanlike, loaded deep with textiles, cutlery, steel and machinery for the insatiable markets of the east. Here was a troopship, painted white, over whose decks and rails a thousand khaki figures swarmed jacket-less, collar-less, but wearing still (as regulations demanded) the topees issued them at Port Said – jolly fellows they looked, a credit to the Old Country, who waved and whistled as they saw you standing there, while their officers from their deck-chairs amidships smiled genially or raised a glass.

And here, grandest and most symbolic of all, was one of the famous P & O liners of the eastern route, elegantly black of hull and funnel, its bridge shady with white canvas awnings, its decks bright with sunshades and summer frocks. Such a vessel, at 7,000 tons or more, towered regally above the desert there, and sailed imperially indeed down the Lifeline of Empire. Gentlemanly commissioners of Nazipore or Mandalay studied annual reports on her sun-decks. Memsahibs, lightheartedly awry, threw deck quoits or played shuffleboard in the sunshine. Perhaps a gust of laughter reached you from the gaggle of girls larking about with their young men on the poop – girls of the unkindly nicknamed 'fishing-fleet' no doubt, off to find a husband in the Indian Civil Service or the Bengal Lancers.

An air of immensely practised consequence hung about such a ship, an imperial liner treading a familiar imperial course: in her presence, it seemed, were embodied not only the virtues of authority, horsepower and seamanship, but moral certainties too, the certainty that Helen would not cheat at the bridge table, that Roger would be correctly dressed for dinner, that the girls on the poop would go no further than innocent flirtation – not to mention the absolute conviction that if, by some unprecedented catastrophe, the liner were to sink there and then in mid-canal, women and children would be first into the boats.

Several thousand such vessels were sailing the imperial trade routes (the *Titanic* was not built until 1912, but the *Campania*, on the Atlantic run, had already reached 12,950 tons). They comprised more than half of the entire world's merchant fleet, and were lovingly represented by imperial cartographers on maps of international commerce. But though the Red Duster was a familiar signal in every corner of the oceans, up muddy Irrawady creeks, into icy Arctic gulfs, still British seamen need seldom feel far from home. Everywhere along the sea-routes were distributed British ports, docks, coaling stations and naval bases, constructed on tropical headlands, on Pacific capes, on Australasian inlets, and particularly on islands.

The island motif was essential to the spectacle of Empire. The British possessed islands by the hundred, ranging from the Channel Islands off the coast of Normandy which were the oldest and most familiar of their overseas possessions to newly acquired islands of the Pacific which hardly one Briton in a thousand could put a name to. Wherever the sea-routes led them, sooner or later those ships would come across a British island, and it was likely to possess a particular island quality, an imperial intensity of islandness, which was common to them all.

There it lies to port now, the generic Imperial Island, and though it may be steaming and fretted in the equatorial heat, or bundled against the Atlantic cold, still it looks, as we approach the lighthouse on its harbour mole, unmistakably disciplined. No raucous bum-boats jostle us, only the dapper pilot comes aboard from his no less dapper launch, and as we enter the harbour the waterfront buildings all around seem to greet us with a cool if not chilly sort of condescension, being built of the island's white coral, perhaps, or prosperously painted clapboard. The little town is clustered against the hill behind, dominated by the pinnacled tower of its parish church, and there are splodges of green park on the slopes above, and a few pleasant villas scattered here and there in gardens on the outskirts. If there is, it is true, a certain raffish or even slummy suggestion to the shanties, lean-tos and tumbled tenements into which the promenade degenerates at its edges, and if the cab-horses at the pavement below do look rather bonier than one might wish, there is reassurance in the sight of the two smart colonial policemen awaiting us on the quayside, and at least the cabs are marshalled in a seemly queue. Besides, from the yard-arm of the flagpole above the Customs House (nicely Georgian, by the way) the Union Jack flies as a guarantee of common-sense and punctual meal-times.

For if there was one essential element to your British island, it was the imperial element. This is hardly a place at all in its own right, only an infinitesimal link in the long chain of Empire. Its inhabitants may be black, brown or yellow, Christian, Muslim or pagan, but they are primarily subjects of the Queen. High on the hill above the town the mansion of their Governor stands in testimony to this truth, all verandahs, French windows and mansard roofs, with its own Union Jack in the garden, and antique brass cannon just to be seen gleaming on its terrace. Beyond the Customs House the Royal Navy's base is a little warren of docks, warehouses, yards and rope-walks, supervised by a stately clock-tower. And as likely as not, spick-and-span at her moorings below Admiralty House there lies the flagship of the local squadron, painted tropical white perhaps, with the admiral's steam-barge scurrying importantly from ship to shore, and if we are lucky the ship's band just tuning up on the quarter-deck for a rehearsal of tonight's gala concert.

It is abroad, but to us Britons not altogether abroad. So much is familiar, so much is ours, from the patrician presence of that pro-consul on his hill-top to the red pillar-boxes of the Royal Mail upon the foreshore, the names of the banks, companies and agents upon the office fronts, or the particular sprawl of the off-duty sailors outside the café by the landing-stage. The raggety and emaciated porters who now swarm aboard do not look, one must admit, *absolutely* British: but still, bred as they are to God-knows-what superstitions and unhygienic habits, they too are subjects of Her Majesty and so, in a manner of speaking, fellow-citizens of ours.

At the end of every imperial sea-route, at the end of the island chain, an imperial sea-port awaited the ships of Empire. Even at the turn of the twentieth century most of the principal cities of the British Empire were ports, for whether a territory was a colony of white settlers, like Canada or Australia, or a colony of subjected peoples like India or the Gold Coast, the imperial presence was clustered most thickly by the sea. Some of the port-cities were very splendid – those in the subject territories rich and vigorous, those in the white settler colonies often far outshining the dingy industrial cities of the Mother Country (as the colonists had long been conditioned to call the island from which they had generally been so delighted to escape).

Bombay, the chief terminus of the India route, was generally considered the finest city in Asia. It was built upon a series of islands, connected by causeways, which separated the great sheltered harbour of Bombay from the open sea. On the western shore a tremendous series of Government buildings, red-brick and formidable, looked out to the Indian Ocean; on the eastern shore the docks and warehouses were complemented by the premises of the Royal Bombay Yacht Club, and in 1902 by the mammoth turreted presence of the Empire's biggest hotel, the Taj Mahal. Within these imposing ramparts lay the old trading centre of the city, the museums and the colleges, the parks, the Sailors' Rest Home and all the ancillaries of a Victorian sea-port, while to the north there ran away, in decreasing gradations of ostentation, the mills, factories, tenements and shanty-settlements of industrial Bombay.

Urbs Prima in Indis was the civic motto, and it was true that in the course of the Victorian century Bombay had outstripped its rivals, Calcutta and Madras, in wealth, in productivity and in commerce. Especially since the opening of the Suez Canal, Bombay had flourished amazingly. But the more earnest of the imperialists were proud of it for different reasons, for in its development Bombay had honoured the very latest concepts of Victorian urbanism, and stood there as a model of enlightened administration. Carefully planned, diligently watched over by a Civic Improvement Trust, Bombay was rich in parks and gardens and public pleasure places, and by the 1860s its death rate was lower than London's – Florence Nightingale once dryly observed that soon Englishmen would be going out there for their health. It showed what Empire could do. It was enough to make an Englishman's heart beat faster, wrote the late Victorian journalist George Steevens. It was the noblest monument of British enterprise in the world, wrote his contemporary W. S. Caine. (It was an architectural Sodom, wrote Robert Byron half a century later).

Seven thousand miles away, at the end of the Australia route, there stood the city of Melbourne, the proud capital of Victoria Colony. Bombay was unmistakably a colonial metropolis, but Melbourne even then was more like the capital of an independent country, an English *alter ego*. Though it had built its fortunes upon the burly give-and-take of mine and sheep range, and always had its fair share of toughs and layabouts, still it was very aware of its own consequence, and looked down upon all its Australian rivals, Sydney in New South Wales Colony, Brisbane in Queensland, Adelaide in South Australia, Perth in the west, as settlements of hicks, provincials or the criminal classes. Melbourne had never been a penal settlement, and was proud of its unimpeachable origins.

Proud of its decorous progress, too. It had an extremely Anglican Anglican cathedral, and a marvellously club-like Club, and deciduous trees everywhere in true English style, and a main street, Collins Street, which for convenience, cleanliness and handsomeness was locally thought to be at least the equal of Bond Street. The boys of Scotch College were as thoroughly public-school as public schoolboys could be, and the villas which ran away beyond the tree-lined Yarra River towards the seaside promenades of Brighton or Rosebud were nothing if not tasteful, with the stained glass windows on their stairs, their white conservatories, the coaching prints that decorated their smoking-rooms and the barouches which, at least when times were good in the volatile Australian economy, habitually waited in the gravelled drive outside.

Then at the end of the eastern route, hammering, beavering, seething on its hilly island off the Chinese coast, like a magnet of opportunity stood the city of Hong Kong, 'Fragrant Harbour' in the vernacular. If Bombay stood for the fructifying zeal of the Empire, and Melbourne for its social progress, Hong Kong was the very emblem of its greed. It had been acquired by force, and it thrived by cunning, the British businessmen of the place having made their wealth by the skilful manipulation of the Chinese opium trade, and maintained it by a stranglehold upon the rest of Chinese commerce. By High Victorian times they had built a Gothic cathedral prominently above their waterfront, as if to announce their reform, but in fact they and their town were almost as cut-throat as ever.

A constant sense of fizz, laced with conspiracy, enlivened the streets of Hong Kong. Half Chinese, half British, altogether capitalist in the era of free trade and market values, it was a standing reminder that in this empire as in most others, avarice was the first and guiding motive. That tower of St John's might stand respectably above the strand, and around it all the paraphernalia of Victorian order, law court and barrack, club and Government House, might dutifully be grouped: but this was a skuldug city really, where the evangelical responsibilities of empire sat lightly upon the merchants' shoulders, and the price of gold was more closely regarded than the cost of glory.

And on the other side of the Pacific, at the end of the longest imperial trade route of them all, the infant city of Vancouver grew beside its landing-stages all bounce and promise. It had been in existence for only thirty years, since Captain 'Gassy Jack' Deighton, retiring from the sea, had opened his popular saloon beside the lumber-wharf, but already it seemed destined for great things. To its quaysides the gold came down from Yukon, the timber from the forests of the interior; the tracks of the Canadian Pacific Railway were already laid to the bottom of Howe Street, and the city fathers looked forward eagerly to the opening of the proposed Panama Canal, which would halve the sailing time to the East Coast and Europe, and make them all rich.

Settlers in their thousands, half of them Scots, were now thronging the shores of Vancouver Bay, and the city was expanding almost before one's eyes. A thriving Chinatown had come with the railway, and built its shops and houses around Dupont Street; to the west posher purlieus were beginning to acquire cachet and resale value; and though most of the buildings were still of wood, and the more uncouth older inhabitants would insist on calling the place by its original name of Gasville (after Captain Deighton), still electric tramcars were already running along Cordova Street, hotels and offices were springing up everywhere, and down on Water Street, overlooking the bay and the snow-capped mountains beyond, the Hudson's Bay Company had built itself a splendid five-storey warehouse, the tallest building in western Canada, which expressed in its fine brickwork and Romanesque arches the very spirit of commercial confidence. If Vancouver had a civic motto, it might well have been the epitaph which Gassy Jack himself had caused to be carved upon his tombstone: '*I have done well since I came here.*'

Beyond those thriving ports lay the opportunities of empire. Australian outback, Canadian prairie, Indian plain, African forest or plateau – the cities were only gateways to the imperial hinterlands, so rich in trade and minerals, where the pioneers and advance guards explored, worked, fought and traded.

Yet often enough the deepest emotions of the imperial activists were tugged back along the seaways, back through the islands to the Mother Country. Homesickness, regret, patriotism, frustration, ill-health, even a touch of envy perhaps, kept its memory fresh in their minds. Sydney might be fine, there was money to be made in Cape Town, Toronto was unarguably The City Of The Future, but still there was nowhere like London after all. London was the start and finish of all these far-flung routes, and the British Empire was unchallengeably capped by this astonishing and unforgettable city.

It was scarcely an imperial city, even then, in the way that Rome had been. Indeed it did not look as conventionally imperial as Paris, with its grandiloquent boulevards, or Berlin with its heroic trophies, or even the symbol-laden Washington. London's growth over many centuries had been scarcely interrupted by war or revolution, and only peripherally affected by the acquisition of empire. It was a profoundly organic city, unplanned, which had become almost despite itself one of the great industrial, diplomatic, financial and artistic centres of the world. London was a vast and foggy confusion. Smoke-blackened, damp, fusty, vital, it extended from its monumental centre as far as the eye could see, far into the green countrysides of Surrey, Middlesex, Kent or Essex, in countless rows of terraced houses, line after line, suburb after suburb, giving the whole place, on the ground as on the map, an unfathomable complexity.

Yet at the heart of it, at the end of the nineteenth century, the sense of empire was unavoidable all the same, and made all visiting colonials feel that ultimately it was their capital too. When Queen Victoria came to the throne, in 1837, few Britons thought much about empire. The American colonies had been lost: the heterogenous possessions that remained seemed to many sober analysts more trouble than they were worth. 'The truth is', one of those China merchants wrote to a colleague after a visit home, 'the people appear to be so comfortable in this magnificent country that they cannot really be brought to think of us outlanders . . .' But half a century had passed since then; the Empire, so uninteresting in 1837, had become a national obsession; the scattered territories of Victoria's accession had become the unimaginable holdings of her jubilee; so absolutely had British attitudes changed that by 1897 Joseph Chamberlain, Secretary of State for the Colonies, could declare that without an empire 'England would no longer be the England we love'.

And so London had become the capital of a quarter of the world. Through the grime now oriental splendours gleamed, and frontier prospects beckoned. The great companies of empire gave a new excitement to the City – the shipping houses, the mining firms, the colonial banks. The headquarters of the colonial agents brought new freshness to the Strand. Posters advertised cheap passages to the Klondyke or the Rand, statues commemorated imperial worthies here and there, from the windows of the East India Club or the Oriental brown whiskered faces looked bleakly out into the drizzle. Over the green of St James's Park the offices of Empire loyally faced the palace of Monarchy.

And down at the jetties of Tilbury or the East India Docks the ships of the sea-routes came and went: *Ormuz* from Aden and Bombay, *Silver Queen* with mixed cargo for Singapore, *Peewit* recognizably battered after a rough passage from St John's, with her fo'c'sle rail buckled by the Atlantic seas, and a bit of a dent amidships.

Imperial roads: top, Threadneedle Street, London; above, the new road at Pangi, India *c.* 1876

Scenes of shipboard life, 1890s

Going Ashore and Coming Aboard. Transhipping passengers by rope and basket,
Port Elizabeth, Cape Colony, 1894

'T. Baines and C. Humphrey Killing an Alligator' Thomas Baines, 1856

'The Great Western Fall, Victoria Falls' Thomas Baines, 1863

'Coming South' Tom Roberts, 1886

'Far From Home' John Evan Hodgson, 1889

'The Island of Tristan da Cunha' O. W. Brierly, 1867

The Apollo Bundar, Bombay

Imperial dock scenes: above, Hobart Harbour, Tasmania, *c.* 1870
right, disembarking at Cape Town

Along the trade routes in the 1890s: left, the Phoenix
Salmon Cannery, Steveston, British Columbia; top, loading the
banana boat Jamaica; above, coaling ship, Cape Town

Hong Kong harbour, *c.* 1878: in the foreground, Hong Kong Island, in the background Kowloon and the China hills

On board the SS *Norham Castle*, bound for Cape Town, 1894: deck games and fancy dress

On board the SS *Norham Castle*, bound for Cape Town, 1894: types of imperial traveller

In the Colonies: above, Waiting on the Porch, Cape Town, 1894; above left, The Gold Mine Foreman;
left, Teamsters and Loggers, British Columbia, 1880s

Spring Flood on the St Lawrence River, Canada, photographed by Alexander Henderson (active 1859–90)

CHAPTER THREE

LIVING LEGENDS

Cecil Rhodes (1853–1902)

I n many ways the British Empire, standing there so complacently at the pinnacle of its success, was an empire in the mind. Until the middle of the nineteenth century it had not existed in this sort. In those days it was a down-to-earth affair, but a diverse succession of visionaries had given it a metaphysical dimension: politicians, who saw it as a patriotic excitement and an electoral winner; traders and industrialists for whom it promised Eldorado; evangelical Christians, who clothed it in piety; writers and painters, who dressed it up in art; above all the new popular press, circulating among a newly literate populace, which presented it as the greatest of all running stories.

So it was. There never was news quite like the news of empire, in the last quarter of the nineteenth century. Hardly a month passed without some thrilling development in the imperial field. The British fought wars against the Ashanti, the Kaffirs, the Afghans, the Mohmands, the Zulus, the Boers, the Egyptians, the Sudanese, the Burmese, the Matabeles, the Waziris – all ennobled by heroic immolation, all to be victorious in the end. The Kings of

'Kitchener of Khartoum' H. von Herkomer, 1890

'General Gordon's Last Stand' G. W. Joy, 1885

Burma had been overthrown, the Kings of Benin had been humiliated, the Asahantahene had been taught a lesson, the Metis of Canada had been put in their place, the island of Zanzibar had been acquired, the colony of Rhodesia had been founded. General Roberts had led his epic march from Kabul to Kandahar, General Wolseley had made the British masters of Egypt, General Gordon had died a martyr's death in his African palace.

This was the stuff of myth, and a kind of instant folklore had developed around the late Victorian empire – part morality play, part *Golden Bough* (a book first published, as it happens, in 1890). Ancient continuities were devised to fit it, champions like Drake, Alfred, Arthur or even Boadicea were offered as progenitors, imperialist poets indulged themselves in classical parallels and mystic metaphors:

> *England! where the sacred flame*
> *Burns before the inmost shrine,*
> *Where the lips that love thy name*
> *Consecrate their hopes and thine . . .*

Fortunately Victorian stalwarts lent themselves admirably to the processes of the collective unconscious, and so the heroes and pro-consuls of the Empire were elevated satisfactorily into living legends.

The heroes were mostly *Golden Bough*. There was, for instance, Dr David Livingstone. This pious but pernickety Scot perfectly combined in his person the saintly and the adventurous strains of empire, and even during his lifetime had been sanctified by the propagandists. In death he went straight into folklore. His sombre countenance looked out from a thousand tracts, his story was told at Sunday schools and prize-givings, medallions of his adventures adorned the frontispieces of adventure stories or the lids of biscuit tins. His birthplace in Scotland became a place of pilgrimage, and his body lay before the high altar of Westminster Abbey. In the imperial mythology he was the Priest-King, journeying always through the dappled forests, attended by faithful black men, carrying on his frail but unbowed shoulders (one of them, as the story-tellers loved to recall, cruelly savaged by a lion) the grand burden of enlightenment.

Then there was the Dying God – General Gordon of course. Gordon was everything a legend-maker could require. His personality was hypnotic. His eyes were a piercing and disturbing blue – 'the eye', as anonymous natives were commonly quoted as saying, 'of a god'. His bearing was military but always modest. His enthusiasms were peculiar perhaps, but decidedly grand: he was a bold identifier of Biblical sites in Jerusalem, a rescuer of souls among the poor of Gravesend, and it was he who had definitively sited the Garden of Eden on the bed of the Indian Ocean near the Seychelles. He had been a guerilla leader in China, acquiring the glamorous cognomen 'Chinese' Gordon, and when a hero was required to extricate the British Empire from a nasty predicament on the Nile, at a few hours' notice he left, borrowing a couple of pounds at Charing Cross to see him through the journey. What more could one ask? Only an apotheosis: and this the general magnificently provided by being stabbed to death with assegais on the steps of his Governor's Palace in Khartoum.

Cecil Rhodes was the Giant of the mythology: a paunchy and slightly suspect giant, but a giant nonetheless. Bad health had driven him to South Africa in his youth, and he had combined an intermittent Oxford career with the making of a great fortune in the Kimberley diamond mines. This wealth he dedicated to Colossal Aims. Not only did he found the eponymous colony of Rhodesia, not only did he launch an All-British railroad from the Cape of Good Hope to Cairo, but he also instituted at his old university the Rhodes Scholarships, intended to produce a constant flow of British colonials, Americans and Germans programmed to promote the interests of Great Britain and the Empire. Rhodes made his own legend as he went along, almost everything he did being consciously on the grand scale, and even at the end he did his best for the story-tellers: his last words were reported to be 'So little done, so much to do', and his chosen burial-place was away in the bare Matopo hills of Rhodesia, high above the colony he created and the quarrelsome tribes he quelled.

There had to be a Puck in the Wood, and this role was filled by Rhodes's old friend and physician Starr Jameson. When in 1895 Rhodes decided to incite a pro-British rising in the Boer city of Johannesburg, the centre of the Rand goldfields, Jameson led the filibustering raid which was intended to exploit the coup, and which gave his name to the English language. The Jameson Raid was a ghastly flop – the rising failed and the impetuous doctor spent some time in prison – but it did nothing to spoil Jameson's popular reputation, and he instantly entered the fables. London society lionized him, the Poet Laureate wrote a poem about his exploits, and the great public, far from blaming him for the affair, loved him for it: they thought it an adventure of the best mischievous kind, a spit-in-the-eye, singe-the-king's-beard kind of adventure (and within five years the British had seized Johannesburg anyway, allowing Puck to go on to be Premier of Cape Province, a Privy Councillor and a baronet).

The War-Lord of Empire was undoubtedly Herbert Kitchener, avenger of Gordon, defeater of Boers. He was not hard to legendize either, for he lived always by effect. Sometimes people saw through his tremendous façade, but generally they took him at his own valuation, and believed this bullier of Fuzzy-Wuzzies to be one of history's great marshals. His very conceit commanded adoration: even his savage excesses in the Sudan, when he allowed the enemy wounded to be shot on the field of battle, and had a defeated chieftain paraded in chains behind his horse – even these barbaric gestures were thought proper to such a man of battle, stern, terrible and gigantic. When he was Chief of Staff in the Boer War, fighting an army of raggle-taggle irregulars, he rode about the country on his white charger attended by Indian lancers in gilt and scarlet: and when he died he did it in properly Wagnerian style in the ice-cold waters of Orkney, going down with the cruiser *Hampshire* on his way to Russia.

The imperial May-King was perhaps Robert Baden-Powell, who entered the legends after his defence of Mafeking in the Second Boer War, and who became the darling of the public for his jauntiness, his fun, and his imperturbability. A dapper little man, not invariably addicted to the truth and nothing but, Baden-Powell assiduously cherished his own image, even to his nickname 'B-P', and made sure that he and the successful defence of Mafeking were universally synonymous. As a result, his activities there cheered up the whole nation – his famous bluffs and ruses, his always cocky dispatches, his love for fancy dress and amateur theatricals even in the grimmest moments of the siege, his tuneful whistle as he peered through his telescope on his watch-tower at the enemy lines outside. No matter that the siege was not really quite as terrible as 'B-P' implied, and that the British garrison made no real attempt to break out: the very manner of its defence was a victory and an inspiration, and made Baden-Powell, who had been its life and soul, momentarily the life and soul of Empire too.

And in the Fleet was Admiral 'Jacky' Fisher, the Man of the Sea, who had, by the nature of the times, scarcely heard a gun fired in anger, but who was most people's idea of a British fighting admiral. Fisher was a Nelson-worshipper, and emulated his idol in his fascinating mixture of effrontery, tenderness, arrogance, charm and ruthlessness – adding in later years a conspiratorial streak that was all his own. An Englishman of such suggestively oriental cast that rumour alleged him to be the child of an eastern princess, Fisher really came of bourgeois stock, but developed un-bourgeois attitudes. He was outrageous, gossipy, funny, quick to tears or laughter. He loved dancing, and made it compulsory for his officers. He revelled in the company of business magnates, Jews, newspaper proprietors, Americans, kings and duchesses, and in his very presence he was a true personification of the imperial myth. When his Mediterranean Fleet once paid a courtesy visit upon the Sultan of Morocco, His Highness was asked afterwards what had impressed him most about the spectacle – the guns, the drill, the paintwork, the great warships themselves? 'Admiral Fisher's face,' he said.

The pro-consuls of Empire, on the other hand, were distinctly Morality Play, and were imagined generically, in their distant palaces, as grave, just, powerful and preferably bearded. Many of them in fact, whether they were governors of infinitesimal archipelagos or viceroys of India itself, might not have been thought particularly interesting applicants if considered for the board of a jam manufactory, but a few among them really were proper matter for allegory.

There was Evelyn Baring of Egypt for a start, commonly known as Over-Baring until his elevation to the peerage as Lord Cromer. He was a man of profound and awful seriousness, the very antithesis of the light-hearted, volatile, affectionate and not very efficient Egyptians his duty it was to govern. Though in theory his office was no more than that of British Consul-General, in practice his authority in the land was almost absolute, and he exerted it with a Roman air, writing his reports in Ciceronian vein, treating the Khedive of Egypt *de haut en bas*, and moving about Cairo in tremendous state, preceded by barefoot runners with wands like the bearers of fasces. His professional views were uncompromising. When asked once if Egyptians ought not to be allowed to govern themselves, he replied simply that 'they should be permitted to govern themselves after the fashion in which Europeans think they ought to be governed' – the imperial morality at its starkest.

Slightly younger than Cromer, though certainly no less imposing, was Lord Curzon the Viceroy of India, known to the educated public then, and perhaps best remembered even now, for a scurrilous rhyme attached to him at Oxford:

> *My name is George Nathaniel Curzon,*
> *I am a most superior person.*
> *My cheek is pink, my hair is sleek,*
> *I dine at Blenheim once a week.*

Curzon was brought up in the ancestral home of Kedleston Hall in Derbyshire, and was gratified, when appointed Viceroy in 1898, to be able to move into a palace in Calcutta which was an architectural copy of his own house. He was very much at ease in the viceregal office, immensely enjoying the stately grandeur of the job, riding about on elephants as to the manner born, and holding himself in very haughty and pictorial postures (he had a bad back, and was painfully corsetted always). He infuriated Indians by some of his high-handed policies, but at the same time he developed a deep admiration for the Indian cultures, and grew to abhor the stuffy convention-ality of Anglo-Indian life – living in Simla, he said, was like dining every day in the housekeeper's room with the butler and the lady's maid. He really was, as the rhyme said, a very superior person. When in 1912 he suspended the home leave of one of the smartest British cavalry regiments, the 9th Lancers, because he suspected them of complicity in the murder of an Indian, almost the whole of Anglo-India excoriated him for it: but he did not care, and in the high imperial style shrugged it off with the remark that nothing was so satisfying as 'the consciousness of having done the right'.

In Africa there was Frederick Lugard, whose personality was presented to the public as a cross between Livingstone and Rhodes. He did not much look the part, actually. A small, rather wispy sort of man, with drooping moustaches and beady eyes, he nevertheless was the true begetter of two great colonies, Uganda and Nigeria, and almost alone among the pro-consuls, had evolved an imperial ideology. He saw the Empire as a gigantic exchange, in which British skills could be swapped for the resources of the subject peoples: the system should be administered by indigenous leaders, supervised by British officials playing the part of school prefects to promising younger boys. It was a kindly, if patronizing, attitude to empire, but then Lugard was a kindly man. His contribution to the imperial scene was schoolmasterly but benign, and an entire strain of the imperial condition could be summed up by a glimpse of him in the field: a neat upright figure, dressed in white ducks and a straw hat, dominating nevertheless the fantastic assembly of African chieftains towering over him with their gorgeous robes and feathered whisks, their ivory staves of office and their not necessarily ceremonial clubs.

In some people's eyes Lord Milner, British High Commissioner in South Africa, was the imperial authority incarnate. Born and raised in Germany, he brought to the matter of empire a harder, clearer analysis than was common in that emotional heyday – the cleverest man perhaps, but probably not the wisest, ever to govern a part of the British Empire. 'In Egypt', he said after a spell of service there, 'there is no argument but "you must"', and his conviction of command was positively blazing. He believed in the establishment of a British super-state, embracing within one political entity all the white subjects of the Empire, and sustained by the wealth of all the coloured ones. In fact almost all his policies failed, and almost all his ideas proved deluded: but in the climax of his career, which coincided more or less with the climax of the Empire, he seemed a man of irresistible mastery, 'flowing', as he said himself, 'from head to foot with one . . . mass of conviction'.

Over-Baring, Superior Person, the Schoolmaster, Conviction: and here finally is a character who, though a plenipotentiary himself, in a way most nearly filled the part of Everyman in this drama. Francis Younghusband became famous in 1902 when he led a British expedition to Lhasa in Tibet – the ultimate extension of imperialism, romantics thought, bringing the long arm of British order into the most obdurate of all the countries of the world. A political officer of the Indian Government, Younghusband was a determined expansionist, believing that the Tibetans were 'not a fair people to be left to themselves', but he was a mystic too, as Everyman must be. He trusted in inner lights, universal brotherhoods, visions and redemptions, and was moved by the Himalayan mountains as by incarnations of the Godhead.

He undertook the invasion in high imperialist spirits, killing several hundred Tibetans in skirmishes along the way, and obliging the Dalai Lama to sign a treaty of abject subservience. He returned, though, a dedicated man of peace, and became celebrated then as the one dreamer to emerge from the imperial experience. For before his mission left Lhasa for the long return march to India, Younghusband climbed a hill outside the capital and looked back at the shining mass of the Potala palace on its hill. There and then he experienced a moment of ecstasy, like a religious experience –'never again could I think evil, or have an enmity with any man'. He obeyed the revelation, never went to battle again, and devoted the rest of his life to reconciliation, geography, peaceful adventure and contemplation.

These folk-images, and many others, were more or less worshipped in those superstitious decades of the imperial climax: but nobody received so many offerings, was danced around so devotedly or invested with such mystery, as Queen Victoria herself, the presiding totem of the whole ritual. Removed from her astonishing circumstances she might not have seemed very striking: a small, rotund German matron, dressed in her old age entirely in black, with a moderate gift for sketching, a tiresome susceptibility to ghillies and Indian footmen, and a rather sullen turn of countenance. History, though, fervently assisted by the imperial magic-men, had transformed her. She had acquired an arcane fascination, and came to look indeed rather like a stumpy idol of some sort, a stylized fetish, a candle-blackened Madonna. She seemed to be of no particular nationality, of no particular race even, slumped as she was there beneath her parasol in her widow's weeds, and there was no mistaking *her* place in the mythology: the Great White Queen, the Queen-Across-The-Water, the fount of honour, the protector of goodness, the searcher-out of evil, whose image was known in every corner of the world, and whose name was to be perpetuated in capes, bays, provinces, cities, lakes, islands, mountains and railway stations everywhere.

Sometimes, just occasionally, the Queen-Empress was seen to smile. It was a surprisingly sweet and girlish smile, and it illuminated not only her face, but her entire being. She was seen to be ageless then, like any other Earth-Mother.

Top left, David Livingstone (1813–73); left, Francis Younghusband (1863–1942); right, Frederick Lugard (1858–1945)

Queen Victoria (1819–1901) works at her dispatch boxes, 1893

Rhodes the Colossus: above left, in middle life with the officers of a Highland regiment in South Africa; left, at the height of his power, with Joseph Chamberlain (1836–1914), Secretary of State for the Colonies, in attendance seated right

Above, Leander Starr Jameson (1853–1917), fourth from left, standing, with other officers of the Jameson Raid.
Right, Evelyn Baring (1841–1917), as British Agent-General in Egypt

George Nathaniel Curzon (1859–1925), as Viceroy of India: above right, with the Nizam of Hyderabad on an official progress; right, with Lady Curzon on a tiger shoot

Left, John Fisher (1841–1920), as captain of HMS *Excellent*, 1883.
Above, Alfred Milner (1854–1925), as British High Commissioner in South Africa, 1901

Above, Charles Gordon (1833–85). Right, Herbert Kitchener
(1850–1916) after the taking of Johannesburg, 1900 (the officer in
the centre is Ian Hamilton, 1853–1947, later to be the unsuccessful British
commander of the attack on the Dardanelles, 1915)

CHAPTER FOUR

THE BUILDING ART

The Secretariat Building, Kuala Lumpur, Federated Malay States

Picture a representative building of the British Empire, silhouetted for us against the glow of that old spectacle, and we are likely to imagine some romantic fantasy of Oriental Victorianism, part western, part eastern, bulbous dome beside pinnacled turret, standing in showy display beneath cloudless sky or swirling monsoon cloud. And we are right, for something of the sort really was the nearest the British ever got to an imperial style of architecture. They had run through a whole gamut of modes in the attempt – classical pastiche in India, Australian Georgian, the lovely Colonial architecture of Canada's eastern seaboard, transplanted Palladian, even tropicalized Early English. This fine variety was never destroyed: but it was overlaid, sometimes overwhelmed, and in a sense sealed by the triumphant eclecticism of the Victorian climax.

The British were not great builders in the Roman or the Spanish kind – they erected few colossal memorials to their own grandeur, few triumphal staircases or epic temples. That was not their way. Their Colosseum was only the station racecourse, their Pantheon the modest Anglican cathedral, and the palaces of their pro-consuls were, by and large, hardly more than comfortable gentlemen's residences. But the profusion of their buildings was unexampled. The architects of the British Empire, often amateurs, really did alter the face of the earth: never in history had one people distributed its constructions so lavishly, or stamped its taste so ineluctably across the continents.

The forms varied, of course, not only from decade to decade, but from territory to territory, climate to climate. So did the building methods and materials. Let us consider then a few of the more characteristic building types through which the Empire struggled towards an architectural fulfilment.

Take first the Anglo-Indian bungalow. This was a true vernacular of empire. It was based upon Indian models but by Victorian times had become emblematically British. Basically a simple single-storey structure surrounded by verandahs, it had evolved into myriad derivatives, and ranged in appearance from the utterly functional to the floridly ornamental, in purpose from the cowshed to the divisional headquarters, in location from its original Bengal to Aden, Penang, South Africa or even Jamaica, and in comfort from the austere single-room-and-bathroom of the up-country lodging to the luxurious interconnecting series of white pavilions, embellished with elegant woodwork, which served as an urban retreat for the Governor of Bombay.

The bungalow by then was an instructive illustration of the imperial method. It was surrounded nearly always by a compound, insulating the sahibs from their sometimes insanitary and occasionally tumultuous subjects; and within its garden too it was a little microcosm of empire, the European domestic quarters being altogether separate from the kitchens and out-buildings allotted to the miscellaneous cooks, bearers, grooms, gardeners, cows, horses or camels thought essential to the imperialist well-being. The house itself was pointedly private, and the big gateposts at the compound entrance, marked so firmly with the owner's name, made it altogether clear to passers-by that this was imperial territory.

Only the verandah, the most obviously Indian part of the house, formed a kind of bridge between the cultures of rulers and ruled – the verandah, itself a metaphor of empire, upon whose *chaises longues* the sahib might relax with his dogs and his sundowner, from whose embroidery frame his wife, so largely denied contact with the dark world of India beyond that compound gate, might at least get some sound or smell of it, and over whose tea-cups now and then, when Mr Mutterjee of Public Works came visiting, or Ahmed Mohammed arrived to give the major his weekly Urdu lesson, Britons and Indians met as human beings.

At another level of imperial domestic life was the Governor's mansion, generically known as Government House, which varied in consequence from the tremendous palace of the Viceroys at Calcutta, one of the great houses of the east, to the seaside villa of the Administrator of St Lucia in the Windward Islands, which stood above the bay at Castries like a well-recommended family boarding-house. Between these two extremes, at the turn of the twentieth century, a multitude of comfortable, generously proportioned, lawn-embowered residences flourished in rigid protocol from one end of the Empire to the other. In every possession, great or small, Government House was the focus of social life. The Governor (or Viceroy, or Lieutenant-Governor, or Administrator, or even in the case of Lord Cromer simply Consul-General) was the Queen's personal representative, the shadow of the Crown: men wore their top hats and medals, when they went to his garden parties, and women practised their curtseys in advance.

Whatever their size and architectural style, Government Houses were notable for a certain sameness of décor. The English country house was the model, and the same sorts of furniture, the same colours of cushions, the same selection of magazines on the sofa-table, the same taste in pictures, was likely to be displayed in Dar-es-Salaam, where Government House was a mock-Moorish palace, in Gibraltar, where it was a converted convent, in Rangoon, where it was a French-Renaissance chateau, or in the Falkland Islands, where it was a tough granite farmhouse. Military trophies were almost *de rigeur* – crossed swords, burnished shields, superannuated cannon on the garden terrace. English sporting prints were essential too, and sometimes victorious treaties were displayed, or the gee-gaws of defeated primitives. Huge portraits of predecessors in office hung in halls and dining-rooms, and propped upon pianofortes were the signed photographs of royal dukes or even princes who had stopped off at Hobart, or Belize, or Aden, during official progresses or holiday cruises.

And the Queen-Empress was there, of course – there in portrait almost certainly, with a crown mounted above her heavy gilt frame, but there more suggestively in proxy. The Government Houses of Empire were not all very regal in themselves. Some were a little vulgar – the viceregal palace erected at Simla in the 1880s was furnished throughout by Maples of London, and would do well, thought Lady Curzon, one of its more fastidious chatelaines, for a Minneapolis millionaire. Some were distinctly unassertive – Government House at Belize, in British Honduras, was a worm-infested clapboard building which might have been a church school or an inadequately-endowed cottage hospital. Some were endearingly pompous – Government House at Hobart, in Tasmania, was just like a Scottish castle, and was even alleged to have acquired, during its brief and altogether mundane history, a couple of authentic ghosts. Some were just awful – Government House at Hong Kong looked more like a detention barracks than a house, Government House at Poona in India was alleged to be a blend of the Renaissance, the Romanesque and the Hindu styles, while if one of the Viceroy of Ireland's official quarters was a lovely house in Phoenix Park, the other was Dublin Castle, the most ominous, ugly and generally detested building in the entire island.

The vicarious presence of Queen Victoria, however, made of them, if not an architectural unity, at least a spiritual ensemble: it could truly be said that, for all the differences between them, if you knew one Government House of the British Empire, in the deepest sense you knew them all.

Somewhere up the road from every bungalow, somewhere very close to Government House, was sure to be an Anglican church. God and Empire went together, at the climax of the evangelical century, and colonial bishops ranked high in the imperial hierarchy. This was not a proselytizing empire – it disclaimed all official intention to convert the heathen (that is, the subject peoples) to the true (that is, the British) faith. It did believe itself, all the same, to be doing God's work, and it demonstrated its own spiritual preferences explicitly enough.

So the Anglican church loomed large everywhere. There were chapels too of course, and Catholic churches, but the Church of England was the church of the Establishment, and so of the imperial authority. Every fair-sized imperial city had its cathedral, and some of them were all you could ask of a fane: Singapore's, for instance, which stood nobly spired and white above the city's central green, and was built very properly by convict labour; or the cathedral at St John's, Newfoundland, which welcomed the ships symbolically into port from its perch above the steep and narrow harbour; or the peculiar building, part Byzantine, part African in style, whose twin towers and flying buttresses proclaimed the faith in a forest clearing at Blantyre in Nyasaland; or the cathedral which George Gilbert Scott built at Lahore in India, and which was a sort of essence of cathedral, close, cloister, cathedral school and all, boiled down from all the best Gothic models at home, and reconstituted faithfully in that dusty city of Islam.

Thousands of lesser churches sustained the far-flung sees, and these by the end of the century had achieved a kind of dutiful uniformity. Not that they were really uniform, though often they were built to standard patterns sent out from England, and occasionally indeed from prefabricated parts: but since they were generally constructed economically, with whatever materials were to hand, and since most of them went up within a few decades of each other, like Government Houses they were remarkably alike in spirit. They were English parish churches without their endowments, without their hoary churchyards, without their ancient lineages of squire and parson, without their long patrimony of Christian craftsmanship. They were like little exhibition churches, run up for the occasion, or even toys of bricks and cardboard.

Each had its simple square tower, or perhaps its homely steeple, and beneath it a *porte-cochère*, to guard against equatorial suns or northern snowstorms, gave access to the gothically pointed porch, which smelt variously of dust, damp or goloshes. Within there was a nave and two aisles, lit by clerestory windows, and there were rows of wooden pews (teak, mahogany, stinkwood, pine, according to the locale), and a big brass eagle-lectern presented by the Mother's Union, 1888; and above the altar, its altar-front embroidered by the senior girls of the Anglican School, there was a stained-glass window to commemorate the unflagging attention to duty of a late pastor, perhaps, a well-loved medical officer, a Universally Admired District Commissioner, or Violet Amelia Shepherd, daughter of the late General Sir Hercules Shepherd, KCB, for forty years the devoted organist of this church.

That was all. It was not much, but it had character, and decorum, and integrity. Outside the terrible sun shone down, the fruit-bats played in the gathering dusk, or the snow lay bitter all around.

And talking of snow, if you looked across the frozen river at Ottawa, on a winter day in the 1880s, you would see a very grand new group of buildings crowning the high white ridge of the eastern bank, serene above the log-jams, mills and heaving tugs of the lumber pool beneath. Until a few years before Ottawa had been nothing but Bytown, a cold timber village in the middle of nowhere, but it had been chosen (allegedly by the stab of a hat-pin in Queen Victoria's map) to be the capital of the huge new Canadian Federation, uniting the territories of the imperial north from British Columbia to Prince Edward Island. The great structure up there, representing in masonry the grandeur of this conception, was the new Dominion Parliament: and with its elaborately Gothic outline, its façade based upon the Museum at Oxford and its polygonal library modelled upon the Abbot's Kitchen at Glastonbury, it was an archetypal reflection of the Empire's official aspirations.

'An' archetype, because those aspirations were so confused that even in this high noon of imperial confidence nobody had quite devised a definitive architectural vocabulary to express them. It was relatively easy in Canada. Though the new Dominion had come about by conquest as much as by settlement, and though Canada contained its subdued tribal remnants of the Indian nation, still it was for most purposes a modern European country, self-governing in almost everything. The Ottawa Parliament *looked* like a Parliament, and justifiably suggested, there on that northern bluff, the traditions of Westminster far away.

It was a different matter when it came to those imperial territories which were kept within the fold by the presence, the threat or sometimes the exertion of force. What architectural style could really express a system which combined democracy at home with autocracy abroad? What relevance had Magna Carta to territories ruled by unchallengeable alien decree? How could an architect refer to the Mother of Parliaments, in a country where not a single subject had any kind of vote at all? A home was a home, a Governor was a Governor, a Canada indeed was a Canada, but the elusive ethos of the British Empire itself was devilishly hard to translate into bricks and mortar.

So that Romantic Vision style, the one with the domes and the pinnacles, came fitfully into being. It was evolved properly enough in India, where the contradictions and embarrassments were most obvious. There in the second half of the Victorian century the imperial architects devised a kind of building which, though recognizably imperial in some ways, was reassuringly indigenous in others – a hybrid style which seemed to suggest that Britishness had become organically mated with Orientalism. Dome was allied with half-timber, Gothic porch with Muslim balustrade, and native ornamentation was applied to buildings of strictest imperial purpose.

They gave the concoction a heady variety of names – Indo-Gothic, Saracenic-Byzantine, Renaissance-Moghul – and while purists were always to scoff at the idea, and literary travellers expressed themselves appalled, it did represent an Imperial Style of sorts. It had its tentative precedents perhaps in the Hindu-Gothic whimsy of the Prince Regent's palace at Brighton, or the orientalized mansions which retired nabobs sometimes erected in the English countryside, but in its full flowering it was a true expression of the imperial condescension – as though the Spaniards had built their Andean cathedrals half in the Inca style, or the Romans had incorporated in the buildings of Bath distinct intimations of Stonehenge.

The hybrid idea spread far out of India, and by the 1890s there were imperial buildings tinged with the flavour of many subject cultures – a Parliament at Victoria, British Columbia, that seemed to have pagoda roofs, a Residency at Zomba in Nyasaland that looked distinctly like a kraal, even one or two faintly Chinese bank buildings in Hong Kong. A happy extreme of the principle was reached at Kuala Lumpur, the capital of the Federated Malay States. This pleasant city, hardly more than a mining village fifty years before, was partly Malay, partly Chinese, partly Indian and partly of course British: and the nature of the administration was mongrel too, for the States were merely federated under British suzerainty, and retained their own Sultans. Kuala Lumpur was carefully planned, however, as a capital for them all, and its architectural miscegenations were calculated. The general effect was beguiling. The railway station looked remarkably like a mosque, the Selangor Club was built in pure Tudor, there were Indian sorts of kiosk all over the place.

It was the Secretariat Building, though, the centre of administrative life in Kuala Lumpur, that was the *pièce de resistance*. A long low building of absolute symmetry, this prodigy was a pastiche of mingled Moorish and Italianate, with a tall domed central tower, smaller bobbles right and left, twin external spiral staircases, Arabesque arcades and Cordova brick-work. Tall palm trees emphasized its length and flatness, and enhanced its oriental inferences, but immediately outside its monumental entrance, umpired so to speak by its tower, the members of the Selangor Club habitually played cricket on their pitch of vivid green: and so as one set of imperialists watched the batting more or less from the balconies of the Alhambra, another set looked back, sipping orange squash, from beneath the quaint timber and plaster-work of Merrie England.

On the Verandah: a tea planter's bungalow, Ceylon 1878

Bungalow life in India: above, hill station residence, *c.* 1885;
above right, Reading the News, *c.* 1870; right, Beneath the Trophies, *c.* 1880

Taking it Easy, Doing it the Hard Way: left, tea planter and his bungalow, Ceylon; above, settlers' clearing, Australia

Home Sweet Home: a cob cottage at Canterbury, New Zealand, in the 1860s

The Governor's House, Darjeeling, *c.* 1890

In Jamaica: above, an official residence in the St Andrew's Hills;
right, a public garden in Kingston

The Gubernatorial Style: left, Government House, Calcutta (completed 1803, architect, Charles Wyatt); top, the ballroom, Government House, Calcutta; above, outside Government House, Hobart, Tasmania (completed 1858, architect, W. P. Kay)

Houses of God and Learning: above, the Convocation Hall, Bombay University (completed 1874, architect, Gilbert Scott); above right, Singapore Cathedral (completed 1861, architect, Ronald Macpherson); right, Christ Church, Simla, India (completed 1857)

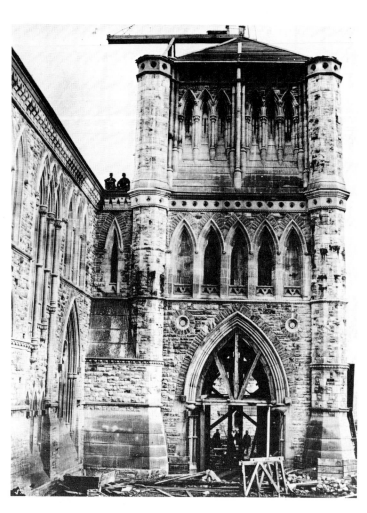

Parliament Buildings, Ottawa (architect, Thomas Fuller):
above, building the main tower, 1863; right, *feu-de-joie* at
the State Opening, 1868

THE VICEROY'S STUDY. VICEREGAL PALACE. SIMLA. 438.

The Gubernatorial Style: above, the study, Viceroy's Lodge, Simla, India;
above left, Viceregal Lodge, Phoenix Park, Dublin, Ireland (completed 1815, architect, Francis Johnston);
left, the Governor's country palace, St Antonio, Malta

CHAPTER FIVE

STEAM, STEEL AND SCIENCE

Crossing the Fraser River, Canadian Pacific Railway, 1899

Far, far out in the Australian outback, beside the waterhole called Alice Springs, one day in the 1890s a miraculous sound was heard. Into the corrugated iron shed that was grandly signed OVERLAND TELEGRAPH OFFICE a chatter of Morse code reached the eager operator, poised at his mechanism upon the rough deal table, watched no doubt in excitement by the Telegraph Manager behind his back. It was a thousand miles to Adelaide one way, a thousand miles to Darwin the other, and until that moment the only communication with the outside world had been by packhorse, camel or prospectors' feet: yet the magical click of the Morse machine that day meant that henceforth Alice Springs, 23°42′S, 133°52′E, was keyed in to an imperial network of modern communications that spanned the earth. When Queen Victoria celebrated her diamond jubilee in 1897, her message to the Empire ('May God Bless My Beloved People') reached Alice Springs from Buckingham Palace in a matter of minutes, through cables that were British all the way, London to Gibraltar to Suez to Bombay to Singapore to Darwin to the remote repeater station of the OVERLAND TELEGRAPH in the outback.

Strewn as it was so randomly across all the continents, the British Empire depended upon technique for its improbable cohesion. It was after all the pre-eminence of the British in the age of steam that had enabled them to acquire this immense hegemony, and which gave them one of their stronger claims to providential duty – somebody, it was reasoned, had to pass on the benefits of scientific discovery to the simpler peoples of the world. Technique also provided much of the spectacle of the British Empire, and wherever the flag flew Steam, Steel and Science fulfilled their own theatrical roles.

It was an engineer's empire. The soldiers and administrators did not like to think so, and technicians, like men of business, were liable to be cold-shouldered at gubernatorial assemblies, or black-balled by posh colonial clubs. Kipling recognized the truth though in his great story *The Bridge Builders*, in which he made the construction of an Indian bridge a metaphor for the building of the Empire itself: while for their own part the imperial engineers considered themselves at least as important as any corps of cavalry or bureaucratic cadre, and often lived in palatial style to match their tremendous works. The existence of the Empire had opened grand new prospects to them, and after the piddling streams and elevations of their own islands they responded with proud flair to the challenges of the far-flung.

Some of their constructions really were among the most ambitious artefacts of the age. Irrigation schemes for instance: these had traditionally been the pride and gauge of empires, providing as they did figures of new fertility, and in their dams and canals the British imperial engineers matched the noblest achievements of the ancients, literally bringing provinces to life, and creating brand-new communities. In Egypt they built the Aswan Dam, claimed to be the greatest of all dams, which subjected the Nile to perennial control for the first time, and distributed its waters through a net of irrigation channels by way of eight lesser barrages. In central India they built the Ganges Canal, claimed to be the greatest of all canals – 800 miles long, with 2,000 miles of feeder canal, crossed by two rivers on aqueducts and by hundreds of road bridges – the whole executed with majestic certainty, and embellished here and there with ornamental lions. In the Punjab they launched the Indus Basin Scheme, claimed to be the greatest of all irrigation works, and intended to provide a grain reservoir for the whole Empire: it watered an area half the size of Britain itself, it was planned to all the latest agricultural and sociological theories, and by the turn of the century the green patchwork of its fields, extending down the Indus river from the foothills almost to the sea, already seemed as perfectly organic as the land itself.

Much the most famous of the imperial roads was the Grand Trunk Road which ran across northern India from one side to the other, from Calcutta on the Bay of Bengal to Peshawar in the marches of Afghanistan. Though much of it had been built originally by the Moghuls, it was completed, rationalized and modernized by the British, and by the end of the nineteenth century was one of the great sights of Empire. Nobody could fail to feel, as they travelled its thousand-mile route across the sub-continent, that this was the work of one of history's prime movers (and nobody could fail to realize, either, how effectively it tightened the grip of the British upon their eastern dominions).

It looked marvellous. Kipling called it 'such a river of life as exists nowhere else in the world'. Generally as straight as a Roman road, most of it was in three lanes, and much of it was shaded by double avenues of trees. It crossed literally thousands of bridges, and tunnelled its way through several mountain ridges, and all along its route, at mathematically regular intervals, were transit camps for troops, lodgings for travellers, police stations and even graveyards. By the end of the Victorian century it was perhaps past its best, for the railways had stolen much of its importance, but still with its undertones of classical precedent the Grand Trunk Road powerfully sustained the imperial stance, and made the British, as they marched along it at the head of their platoons, or trundled down it in horse-and-trap, more proudly British than ever.

Some of the biggest bridges of the day were imperial bridges, and some of the ugliest too, for the last thing the imperial engineers generally thought of was aesthetic appeal. The Lansdowne Bridge across the Jumna river in India, which in its day was the longest single-span suspension bridge in the world, looked less like a bridge than an iron-master's junk-yard, while some of the bridges which carried the Canadian Pacific Railway through the Rockies suggested immense piles of brushwood lashed together. Sometimes, nevertheless, the geographical or historical meaning of a bridge gave it a kind of metaphysical grandeur, and in this category the most famous was the steel railway bridge thrown across the Zambezi river beside the Victoria Falls. Never did bridge find such a site, and nearly everyone who went there recognized in it some symbolic meaning or other. It was not very beautiful in itself, but it had been thrown so daringly across the deep ravine, it stood there so defiantly slender against the thick brown foliage of the forest, that it seemed like a philosophical statement, a calm imperial retort to the unreasoning violence of the Falls behind – whose waters thundered always, whose vapours often cast a rainbow thrillingly against the sky, and whose spray sometimes splashed, as in ritual, upon the windows of the passing trains.

———————

The passing trains! Wherever you stood in the British Empire, beside the thundering Zambezi, in Malta or Mauritius, alone with your pack-horses in the Australian desert, a train was quite likely to pass. If there was one mechanism which summed up the imperial attainment, it was unchallengeably the steam railway, and often the spectacle of the Empire itself was no more, no less the spectacle of the train.

Magnificently across Canada streamed the trains of the Canadian Pacific Railway, past that fine parliamentary pile above the river at Ottawa, over those brushwood bridges, down to the sea hardly a stone's throw from the site of Gassy Jack's saloon at Vancouver. It bored through mountains in daring tunnels, it crossed ravines on vertiginous trestles, it streamed with flare of furnace and shower of sparks through the dark western forests. In many ways the railway was the dominant force in Canadian life, in politics, in economics, even in everyday social affairs: and it made of Canada a demographic unity which the United States to the south, where everyone had to change trains at Chicago, did not achieve until the coming of the airlines.

In Australia the railways, since they were built to different gauges in every State, never did achieve such continental cohesion, but they too were a sight to see. Across the wastelands of the south the Perth Express steamed absolutely straight for 500 miles, without a single curve, while up to Alice Springs, when the tracks got there at last, the train called 'The Ghan', after the Afghan camel-drivers who had preceded it on the route, was sometimes delayed for weeks at a time by floods, but nevertheless looked, chugging so resolutely across those blank and friendless wastes, a very instrument of colonial doggedness.

In Africa Cecil Rhodes saw his Cape-to-Cairo line as an essential part of his megalomaniac view of history. Though it never in fact happened, still up and down the continent lines appeared which were part of the grand design. That bridge beside the Victoria Falls was a link in Cape-to-Cairo, and Rhodes himself had insisted that the trains pass close enough to get the spray upon their carriages. In the north General Kitchener, laying a line into the Sudan for the convenience of his conquering armies, thoughtfully built it to the same gauge as the South African railways, and in the east the audacious Uganda Railway, nicknamed the Lunatic Line, climbed laboriously from the sea to the Uganda highlands as a putative feeder line (and was delayed for several months by man-eating lions who saw it in a similar light).

Down in the south the line across the South African plateau – the Karoo – played a vital part, as Rhodes had foreseen, in the extension of the Empire into the interior, not least in the actions of the Second Boer War which, between 1899 and 1902, established British authority over their implacable rivals the Afrikaners. Then the railway trains discovered a new and sadder kind of symbolism. Railhead frequently became, in that horribly drawn-out conflict, in effect Empire-head: and in the cruel battles of the veldt, when British soldiers were often pinned down for hours at a time by the fire of the enemy entrenched invisibly to their front, tantalizingly behind them they could often see the black smoke of the troop-train that had brought them to their miseries, re-fuelling a mile or two behind the fighting-line, or worse still chugging away in the distance back to the security of the Cape.

And of course the imperial railways were most imperial of all in India. The grandest of the Indian railway stations, Victoria Terminal at Bombay, was thought by connoisseurs to be the grandest station anywhere. 'V.T.', as everyone called it, certainly was majestic in a different way from the neo-classical palaces put up by the railway engineers in Europe or America, because its symbolisms were much more complex: designed by F. W. Stevens, Commander of the Most Eminent Order of the Indian Empire, it proclaimed not only the glory of engineering, as they habitually did, and of financial enterprise, probity, responsibility and the other standard nineteenth-century virtues, but also the more ornamental merits of sovereignty. It looked partly like an Oxford college, but partly like an oriental fantasy, and if it had frescoes of steam engines upon it, and portrait medallions of the directors of the Great Indian Peninsular Railway Company, it also had monkey-gargoyles, sculpted elephants and rampant lions in sentinel. It was truly a depot of dominion, and from it, along the 25,000 miles of the Indian railway system, the authority of empire seemed to flow.

By the end of the century the lines had reached every corner of India, from the sea-ports to the Himalayas. A huge community of workers, mostly Eurasian, lived to keep the trains running, and whole towns arose to service them. There were railway stations of every size, kind and degree of comfort. Some were so isolated that there was no settlement in sight at all. Some were the showiest buildings in town. Some, especially in the volatile regions of the north, were fortified against subversion: a station like Lahore's might look castellated simply for picturesque effect, but those fancy towers really were gun-blocks, those arrow-slits were designed for enfiladed musket-fire, and the massive portcullis at each end of the platform could be lowered at a stroke. Other stations again, especially those in the foothills, were less like stations than cottages ornés: sweet little structures with trellises and potted flowers, which came to life with a start only when, far down in the wooded valley below, the 10.10 from Kalka or Coimbatore could be heard wheezily on its way.

The Indian railways were earnests of comfort and efficiency in an all too often feckless world: amongst all the imperial imagery, nothing was more powerful than the prospect of a distant train speeding across the Indian plains, seen from the wild mountains of the north – its steam flying like a defiance across the flatlands, the distant glint from its windows speaking of ice, newspapers, some decent company at last, the first sitting for dinner and the promise of a bath in Calcutta on Monday morning.

It was the steam above all that did it. The internal combustion engine came too late to enter the mythology of the British Empire, electricity was never much more than a blessed convenience, but steam was fundamental to the imperial style – or rather Steam, for the imperialists themselves always recognized its capital place in their order of things.

In 1872 the British launched a campaign against the ferocious, able and secretive kingdom of the Ashanti, in Nigeria. The imperial army was led by the most respected of its commanders, General Sir Garnet Wolseley, Gilbert's 'very model of a modern major-general', and was equipped with all the latest devices of colonial warfare, like heat-respirators, cholera-belts, hospital ships and war correspondents. Before launching his assault, however, Wolseley gave the King of the Ashanti one last chance, by sending him an ultimatum and offering him some not very conciliatory terms.

This the general did in a truly imperial way. He did not, as generals more often did, send his demands by the hand of a dashing cavalry officer. Nor did he, as other imperial conquerors had, fire his ultimatum out of a cannon. Instead he gave it to an Ashanti prisoner, and this trembling emissary he sent off towards the enemy lines on the rear platform of an all-British, brass-bound, steam-powered Locomotive Traction Engine.

Empire itself went hissing and thumping off into the jungle that day: and though it is true that the Asahantene took not the slightest notice of it, obliging Sir Garnet to fight one of the most generally admired of his wars, still in the end, inevitably, the impertinent resistance of the Ashanti was overcome, and their ancient capital burnt to the ground by Scotsmen.

The Imperial Communications: top, the staff of the Freetown
Post Office, Sierra Leone, West Africa, 1890s; above, men of
the Overland Telegraph, Roper River, Australia, 1872;
right, laying the cable, Botany Bay, New South Wales, 1876

Laying the cable, Botany Bay
FEB. 1876

Empire on the Nile: above, swing bridge at Cairo; right, views of the Aswan Dam
(completed 1900, designer, Benjamin Baker)

Road building in Jamaica

Building an aqueduct in Cape Colony, South Africa

'A Scene on the Great Trunk Road' Jacomb Hood, 1903

'An Indian Railway Station' William Simpson, 1866

'The Great Indian Peninsular Terminus, Bombay' anon, *c.* 1890

' "Fire's On", Lapstone Tunnel, 1891' Arthur Streeton

'The Derby Express', Derby, Tasmania, 1900

The Bridge Builders: left, the Victoria Falls bridge over the Zambezi, Rhodesia
(completed 1905, designer, G. A. Hobson); above, bridge with fisherman, Australia

The Railway Builders: above, scenes during the construction of
the Kandy-to-Colombo railway line, Ceylon, 1866–70; right, crossing
the Santa Cruz bridge, on the Puebla Branch Railway, Trinidad, *c.* 1870

On the Canadian Pacific: above, the arrival of the first train at Vancouver, 1887;
right, wooden bridge over the Scuzzy River, 1881

On the Canadian Pacific: left, Canyon Creek bridge, in the Kettle Valley; above, inside and outside the railway hotel, Field, British Columbia

Railways of the Indian Raj: top, a ceremonial occasion at an
Indian railway station, *c.* 1895; above, the saloon coach built for the
Prince of Wales's tour of India, 1905; right, the loop called
Agony Point on the Darjeeling railway, *c.* 1897·

Steam in Ireland: through the Kerry Hills by the Great Southern and Western

The imperial railways go to war:
top, volunteers for the Second Boer War parading at Sottsdale station, Tasmania, 1900;
above, a train blown up by Boer commandos, South Africa 1900

CHAPTER SIX

SHOW OF FORCE

British Maxim gunners, Ladysmith, South Africa, 1900

Force was the origin, the sustenance and half the effect of the Victorian Empire. It was largely bluff, for though it was true that the British had, as the poet Hilaire Belloc once observed, 'the Maxim gun and they have not', still it was patently impossible for 41 million islanders to keep a quarter of the world in subjection by weight of numbers or *matériel*, or even for that matter by martial skill. That the Empire survived was due as much to the overweening idea of it as to its ships and guns, the fighting qualities of its soldiers or the frequently imperfect strategic insights of its generals.

The armed forces of the late Victorian age, nevertheless, were designed to an imperial purpose. The Royal Navy was enormous, but consisted mainly of scattered small units, not equipped to meet an enemy of similar size or modernity, but very practised at showing the flag or quelling riots with gunboats. The land forces consisted of a small British volunteer army, so often packed off to the colonial wars that it was almost a standing expeditionary force, backed by a large mercenary force, the Indian Army, and by a ragbag of miscellaneous colonial units (dressed up by their masters, incidentally, in a colourful profusion of fezzes, coolie hats, thigh boots, embroidered jackets, braided epaulettes and white gaiters). It was a curious sort of power, all in all, but it was not in the least ashamed of its eccentricities, recognizing them indeed as a sort of weaponry themselves, like the fetishes and ju-jus that its more barbaric opponents carried with them into action.

The Navy's particular pose was proprietorial. It had not been challenged since Nelson's overwhelming defeat of the French and Spaniards at Trafalgar, and by the 1890s it had not only become an unavoidable presence on the world's oceans, but very often behaved as though it owned them. The British in effect regulated the navigation of the world, and they had appropriated the right to exert their naval authority everywhere, if only by being there. When in 1902 the Russian Admiral Rozhestvensky took his poor fleet of antiquated and overloaded battleships from Kronstadt around the Cape of Good Hope to the China Sea, where it was to be annihilated by the Japanese, for thousands of miles he was contemptuously shadowed by the elegant cruisers of the Royal Navy, a couple of which were always somewhere around, showing off their seamanship.

Nelson himself had set this tone of masterly ubiquity, doubling back as he so often did here and there across entire oceans. Nelson indeed, though he had been dead for the better part of a century, set the tone of the whole fleet. He was the star of stars on this particular stage of the imperial theatre, and the Navy was besotted by his memory. As the years passed, it is true, his example had become a little blunted: the blind eye was not encouraged, in the Royal Navy of the 1890s, and recklessness was better kept within the rules. From a force officered predominantly by middle-class men like Nelson himself, men with whom Queen Victoria had once openly asked if it would be proper for her to dine, the Royal Navy had mutated into a service of resplendent social prestige: dukes and earls abounded in its officer corps, royal princes were habitually enlisted, and the general impression of the whole was one of unattainable aristocratic accomplishment.

Still, it was Nelsonic in a sort of puffed-up, overblown way, and was certainly rich in the originals thought necessary to the heritage. Its ratings were robustly rough-and-ready (no knives and forks were used below-deck in the Royal Navy, and the sailors habitually went around barefoot). Its officers could be outrageously unorthodox, and thought of themselves as members of the best of all clubs, descended directly from Trafalgar's band of brothers. The Empire gave them marvellous scope for their foibles, allowing them as it so often did to sail away into remote corners of the globe far from the supervision of the Admiralty. 'Well boys', the captains of British warships used to ask their officers sometimes, as they finished their breakfasts in the sun-splashed wardroom, *where shall we go today?*

Elegance, glitter, tradition were more important than modern fighting efficiency to this unique armed force. Seamanship was a noble skill, and was cherished, but gunnery and engineering were both dirty trades, and generally despised by the officer corps. A ship was judged by its brass-work, not its target practice, and was maintained like a thing of beauty – often the weight of the paint-work affected the speed of a ship, and it was alleged that captains sometimes had ammunition thrown overboard rather than dirty their upperworks by gunnery practice. Yet there was sense to this poppycock, for in imperial terms the appearance of the Navy really was more important than its belligerence: painted white in tropical stations, grey in home waters, the ships of the Royal Navy maintained the imperial power largely by sheer splendour – the scrubbed pine of their brass-studded decks, their impeccable white gun-covers, their gleaming bells and elaborate crests, and the huge white ensigns which, with a languid sort of arrogance, billowed from the tall staffs at their every stern.

At the apex of the imperial age the Royal Navy was distributed in twos and threes everywhere from Bermuda to Hong Kong: the China Station, the South Atlantic Station, the Mediterranean Fleet, the North America Station, the Channel Squadron, the Cape Station, the East Indies Station, the Pacific. In 1897, though, much of it was concentrated in a single enormous squadron for the Spithead Jubilee Review. Here its style was magnificently displayed for all to see – just in time actually, for the world was beginning to shift as the twentieth century approached, the easy assurance of the British was about to fade, and in a few years the fleet would have changed out of all recognition.

Still, just in time it was, to give a thrill of pride to Britons who saw it, and overawe despite themselves foreigners who came to scoff. There the great fleet lay in three lines seven miles long – 173 ships, including more than 50 battleships. They were dressed gaudily overall, their sailors were mustered along their rails, their captains strutted lordly on their bridges high above. In the course of the morning, as it happened, their complacency was momentarily disturbed when suddenly, unannounced and altogether unauthorized, the brand-new turbine steamship *Turbinia* came scudding at 30 knots through the assembled lines – a virtuoso exhibition of marine engineering by

'The Charge of the 21st Lancers at the Battle of Omdurman 1898' Richard Caton-Woodville

'The Battle of Tamai 30th March 1884' Douglas Giles

'Omdurman – The First Battle – 6.30 am 1898' A. Sutherland

Detail from 'The Flight of the Khalifa After his Defeat at the Battle of Omdurman 1898' Robert Talbot-Kelly, 1899

the turbine's inventor, Sir Charles Parsons. It did not matter, though – it was a Nelsonic kind of impertinence after all, thoroughly British, and Sir Charles *was* the son of an earl: and when a little later the Queen-Empress herself sailed down the lines in her royal yacht, all white and gold and Royal Standard, escorted by the Admiralty yacht *Enchantress* and by a liner-load of journalists, far down the mooring-stations the cheers were passed from crew to crew. Sirens sounded, officers saluted, bands struck up, and the reporters on the *Campania* enthusiastically dreamed up their hyperboles: Majestic Monarchs of the Seas, Mighty Leviathans, Guardians of the Lifelines.

The imperial armies were more idiosyncratic still, if only because they were fragmented into hundreds of intricate and introspective segments. This was deliberate. British military theorists believed in the efficacy of tight small loyalties – loyalties sometimes to a technical corps, more often to a regiment, a body of some 800 officers and men bound together by *esprit de corps* and by carefully fostered traditions. It was the opposite of the French and Prussian military systems, which depended upon a universal pride in the army: the British expected unwavering patriotism in their soldiers of course, and loyalty to the Queen went almost without saying, but nobody felt any passion for the imperial armies as such. They were not even honoured with the royal sobriquet, and in most soldiers' emotions amounted to hardly more than often obfuscatory military bureaucracies, somewhere around Whitehall or Calcutta, whose purpose was merely to support the diverse fierce spirits of their separate parts.

In the British Army every corps and every regiment had its own cherished character. The swankiest units, for instance, were the horse and foot regiments of the royal household, the nearest in spirit to the praetorian guards of the continental armies, upon whom they had originally modelled their drills and uniforms. Hardly less lofty were the cavalry regiments of the line, hussars, dragoons, lancers, who were officered by aristocrats too, and who assiduously fostered their not always justified reputations for dash and high jinks. They had esoteric nicknames often – The Bays, The Skins, The Death and Glory Boys, The Delhi Spearmen – and on dressy occasions they wore marvellously theatrical costumes of the cloak, plume and chain-mail kind.

Then there were the determinedly different infantry regiments of the line, a confused gallimaufry of local heritage, family tradition, quirk and legend: kilted regiments of highlanders, whose officers went into battle waving claymores – regiments of Irish Catholics officered by Protestants almost to a man – stalwart county regiments from Yorkshire, Somerset or the Midlands – regiments of randy townsmen, many of them enlisted under assumed names – regiments entitled to wear badges at the backs of their caps, or jackets of curious cut, or esoteric emblems on their lapels, or brown buttons, or double Sam Brownes. Sometimes they were almost like private armies, so close were their associations with particular families or places, and their loyalty to their commanders was often child-like: 'We'll do it, sir, we'll do it!' spontaneously cried the soldiers of the Manchesters, the Devons and the Gordon Highlanders when, during the Second Boer War, Colonel Ian Hamilton assured them they would win, and sent them to their decimation on the field of Elandslaagte.

The gunners, the sappers and the pioneers were just as distinctive, just as proud of their corps, and the morale of the British Army as a whole, especially in the tub-thumping days of *fin-de-siècle*, was invigoratingly high. Foreigners might not think much of so hodge-podge and stagy a force, but then they often did not grasp its functions. It was not intended for mass warfare against conscript armies: except for the Crimean War, the British fought no European enemy during Queen Victoria's reign, and their island army was trained particularly for colonial conflicts. These it fought successfully, on the whole: it faced its black, brown and yellow opponents, generally speaking, from a vantage-point of profound regimental contempt, and usually managed to slaughter them pretty well.

The Indian Army, anyway, was something very different. It was supposed to be the most powerful force in Asia, and in theory at least made of Britain, an off-shore island on the other side of the world, one of the great military Powers of the day. Composed entirely of volunteers, its officers expatriate Britons, this was the force which, in the sensationalist years of the 1890s, more than any other created the imperial image of romantic virility. Its manner was self-consciously exotic. Developed from the armies of the old East India Company, the original British imperialists in India, its most formidable regiments were recruited from the martial peoples of the north, Sikhs, Punjabis, Gurkhas from Nepal, among whom the soldier's calling was the most honourable of all. A leavening of maverick, inherited from the assorted adventurers of the imperial past, expressed itself in the Indian cavalry regiments, some of them more like brotherhoods than military units, whose recruits paid for their own weapons and horses, and whose officers, often the sons of mild English clergymen, disguised themselves marvellously in sashes, sabres and turbans: and what with the pugnacious whiskers of the Sikhs, the swagger of the Punjabi infantrymen, the murderous devotion of the Gurkhas and the swashbuckle of Skinner's or Hodson's Horse, the Indian armies of the Queen were never without panache.

No wonder they were a favourite subject for popular novelists, travel-writers, and later film-makers. Their characters were so often larger than life, from the ramrod colonel, white-moustached and even monocled, to the ever-loyal Sikh subadar or the simple peasant sepoy. It is true that since the Indian Mutiny the Indian Army had never been entirely trusted, was deprived of field artillery and was carefully balanced everywhere by units of the British Army, but still what stylish attitudes it adopted! When it was not clattering with lances and streaming pennants around the Viceroy's barouche, or parading in stately scarlet at a durbar, it was stalking Pathan dissidents from rock to rock of the blistering frontier, or looking out ever-watchful from the ramparts of theatrical forts. The Army of the Raj was in constant performance, and found devoted audiences always.

Spectacular though these armed forces were, and fundamental to the imperial display, there was no pretending that they were infallible. If they always won their wars, they sometimes lost their battles. Generals made fools of themselves, soldiers ran away, battleships occasionally collided. This never distracted the British for long, however, because they had learnt to exploit their defeats as effectively as their victories. A British reverse, they came to imply, was never just a reverse: it was a heroic sacrifice, a brilliant rearguard action, a shameful betrayal, a tragic misunderstanding or very likely a gallant ruse, and on the whole indeed the British cherished their military setbacks more lovingly than their triumphs.

The idea of redemption played a part in this convenient double-think, as it did in the imperial illusion as a whole. Nothing more became the Empire, people thought, than the martyrdom of General Gordon, whose death was really the result of disgraceful indecision and an almost criminal wilfulness. No military action was more fulsomely celebrated than the minuscule defence in 1879 of Rorke's Drift, where a handful of British soldiers, by successfully defending a small compound against the Zulus ('black as hell and thick as grass'), managed to overlay the rather less satisfactory memory of the day before, when 858 Britons and 470 of their auxiliaries had been humiliatingly slaughtered. The terrible disaster at Kabul in 1842, when an entire British army was annihilated by the Afghans, was remembered chiefly because of a poignant painting by the imperialist artist Lady Butler, entitled 'The Remnants of an Army' and showing a solitary exhausted officer, a redemptive figure if ever there was one, appearing on his half-dead pony before the walls of Jellalabad.

For the military style of the British Empire was not all swank and oddity. It contained too essential elements of sacrament. Even at the height of their imperial success, the British liked to imply that the blood of Empire was shed for others. They liked to quote Matthew Arnold on the 'too vast orb' of the imperial burden, and always on their lips were Kipling's lines about the White Man's Burden – *the blame of those ye better, the hate of those ye guard . . .* They were in fact experiencing the only truly militarist phase of their history, the only brief period when the British public at large showed an enthusiastic interest in guns, warships and wars – Alfred Austin the Poet Laureate once remarked that his idea of Heaven was to sit in his garden hearing news of British victories, alternately by land and by sea. They would deny that it was a mere craze, though, inflamed by the penny press and by Jingo politicians. They thought it the revelation of a God-given role: and to this role, if the pomp of martial display was obviously necessary, so was a grand tragedy now and then. The battle honours of the British armed forces did not specify whether actions were victories or defeats –

> *For when the One Great Scorer comes*
> *To write against your name,*
> *He marks – not that you won or lost –*
> *But how you played the game.*

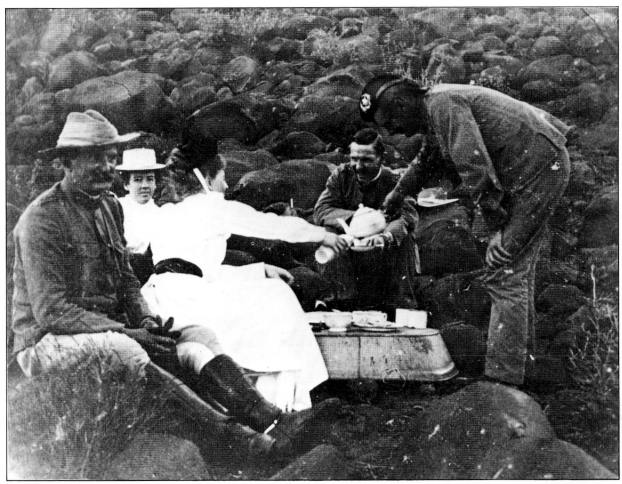

In the field with the imperial armies: top, officers and their ladies at tiffin,
somewhere in South Africa, *c.* 1900; above, among the dead at the battle of Omdurman, 1898

Aspects of naval power: left, ships of the British Pacific fleet
at their base, Esquimalt, Vancouver Island, *c.* 1870;
above, officers of HMS *Eclipse*, West India station, *c.* 1888

Gardiner's Battery, Gibraltar, *c.* 1870; Highlanders on garrison duty

'Queen Victoria's Diamond Jubilee Review at Spithead, 26 June 1897' Charles Dixon

'The Black Watch in the Ashanti Campaign 1874' Richard Caton-Woodville

'H. Melville and Coghill Saving the Colours of the 24th Regiment 22nd January 1879'
Alfonse de Neuville

After the capture of Mindhla, Third Burma War, 1885

Colonel Gardiner, commandant of the Maharajah's troops, Kashmir.
Right, The Indian Army: officers of the 1st Bengal Cavalry;
officers' mess at Peshawar, North-West Frontier

Above, Major Sir Louis Cavagnari, Indian Political Service, with Afghan leaders,
c. 1879, in which year he was murdered during an attack on the British Residency at Kabul.
Left, on the Indian frontiers: resting and riding near the Khyber Pass

Force and the authority of Empire: above, forcible
evictions in Ireland, with battering ram in action; right, officers
and Indian scouts of the Canadian Mounted Police, Alberta

The Second Boer War: left, Canadian volunteers about to embark at Vancouver;
above, the Tasmanian contingent mustered at Hobart

The Second Boer War: above, a Boer commandant,
with the Transvaal flag; left, soldiers of the Leicestershire
Regiment, with a heliograph

The Second Boer War: top, an ox-drawn 12-pounder naval
gun is manhandled into position; above, officers' sword-hilts
and scabbards are painted khaki for active service;
right, Australian volunteers in camp

DINNER TIME CAMP OF BUSHMENS CONTINGENT
KENSINGTON

The Second Boer War: making themselves at home in captured
enemy property are (right) British officers with champagne crate and
native servants, and (above) soldiers of 'Rimington's Tigers',
a corps of locally recruited guides serving with the British Army

The Second Boer War: top, the Leicestershire Regiment withdraws to Ladysmith after its
defeat at Dundee, 1899; above, stretcher-bearers in action in the veldt

'The Surrender of General Cronje to General Roberts of Kandahar at Paardeberg,
with a Guard of Gordon Highlanders' George Scott, *c.* 1900

'Dargai – October 20th 1897', Robert Gibb

'Royal Horse Artillery Crossing a River in South Africa' George Scott, 1900

'Cruel to be Kind' Richard Caton-Woodville, *c.* 1880

The Second Boer War: the victory thanksgiving service at Pretoria, June 8, 1902

CHAPTER SEVEN

IN ART

The Victoria Memorial (sculptor, Sir Thomas Brock, 1911)

Very few Britons, even the most liberal, opposed the imperial idea. It took a prophetic insight, or profound financial understanding, to detect the flaws behind the reasoning. A few political theorists declared the whole thing a mistake, a few economists thought it unprofitable, a handful of moralists believed, even in those intoxicating times, that no one people had the right to rule another. Rudyard Kipling, in the year of the Diamond Jubilee, touched a raw nerve in the nation, but did not deter the imperial progress, with his hymn against *hubris*, 'Recessional':

> *If, drunk with sight of power, we loose*
>   *Wild tongues that have not Thee in awe,*
> *Such boastings as the Gentiles use,*
>   *Or lesser breeds without the Law –*
> *Lord God of Hosts, be with us yet,*
> *Lest we forget – lest we forget!*

It was a vulgar age, a coarsened age, and the bombast of the imperial display well fitted its temper. Besides, the vast majority of the British people believed the Empire to be a force for good in the world – maintaining the peace, improving the natives, and keeping Great Britain itself, God's arbiter on earth, sufficiently rich and powerful to honour His instructions.

During the decades of the imperialist fever almost every national resource was mustered to support these ends: the financial experience of the City of London, the manufacturing capacities of Birmingham or Manchester, the diplomatic skills of British missions around the world, and not least the talents of the nation's writers, artists and musicians, many of whom dedicated themselves to the imperial crusade with an eager and sometimes degraded vigour.

Kiplingesque was the quality half of them aspired to, for already the style and spectacle of Empire had been incomparably captured, and permanently influenced, by the work of the one literary genius of imperialism. If Kipling really had no very clear notion of the imperial meanings, he had an unmatched intuitive grasp of the imperial forms. He was after all a child of Empire, born in India in time to reach artistic maturity at the very moment of the imperial climax, and his view of it all was so bold, colourful and sometimes touching that its appeal spanned tastes and generations, and set the tone of an entire artistic *genre*. All over the British possessions writers took to their pens in the Kipling mode, turning out dialect poems by the thousand, short stories of colonial life from Kuala Lumpur to Hudson's Bay, hundreds of novels with titles like *Jimmy Sahib: A Tale of the Frontier, Duel in the Veldt*, or *The Secret Treasure of Swaziland*.

You could hardly escape the imperial theme in the London publishers' lists. G. A. Henty, and many imitators, thrilled a vast juvenile audience with reconstructions of imperial derring-do, written to a highly commercial formula. Rider Haggard, himself a practising imperialist (it was he who first raised the British flag above the Boer capital of Pretoria), endowed his splendid yarns with a very imperial mystique. Even the great Thomas Hardy almost succumbed, one of his early ideas for an epic poem, later to be fulfilled in *The Dynasts*, being a historical evocation of the British overseas.

The patriotic poets were terrifically high-flown and inflammatory, and achieved great audiences too, their verses generally being rhythmic, easy to remember and chauvinistic. They were mostly armchair Empire-builders. The most virile of them all indeed, W. E. Henley, was a lifelong cripple, but that made his poems all the more inspiring, and gave an added pathos to his anthology of English verse 'commemorative of heroic action'. Sir Henry

Newbolt was another who sang the imperial exploits from afar, but then he managed to collate the whole of the conquering process with the challenges and achievements of English public school life –

> *To set the cause above renown,*
> *To love the game beyond the prize,*
> *To honour, while you strike him down,*
> *The foe that comes with fearless eyes . . .*

Poetic catch-phrases were part of the very atmosphere of imperialism, and there was hardly a literate Briton, at this apogee of Britishness, who could not quote you 'Gunga Din', 'There's a breathless hush in the Close tonight', 'Captain of my Soul' or that well-loved tale of Mad Carew, 'The Green Eye of the Little Yellow God'.

By and large this was a jejune kind of literature, appealing to immature instincts. When it came to Empire even Kipling himself, the presiding genius of this slightly hysterical Parnassus, often wrote below his own best standards. It was boy's art, full of stir and simple principle: and in the evening indeed your young Briton of the day, when he had finished his prep or his homework, found the spirit of Empire expressed in much the same terms in his favourite schoolboy magazine, *Chums, The Captain* or *The Boy's Own Paper*, whose every hero was a stern-jawed Briton, whose villains were habitually black-faced or slit-eyed, and whose inescapable moral was the supremacy of Queen, Flag, Race and Empire.

On the whole painters were more resistant to the imperial spell, so obvious of colour, so swollen of form, but a few did make a speciality of the epic, and their pictures also contributed powerfully to the emotions of the day. Huge specially commissioned oils commemorated the splendours of Indian durbars or royal progressions through the subject lands. Familiar prints of imperial actions, 'Rorke's Drift' or 'Wilson's Last Stand', hung in schools and drawing-rooms across the Empire. They were the ikons of this faith.

They were seldom grand Romantic evocations – not the sort of picture Delacroix would have painted for the British Empire. There was no abandon to them, and blood flowed, if it flowed at all, with a commendable restraint. When a viceregal procession trundled through Lucknow or Agra, in these carefully calculated mementos, all the streets looked preternaturally clean, the elephants never misbehaved themselves, the native populace was uniformly respectful and the Viceroy on top of his swaying howdah was altogether unperturbed. When a general rode into a conquered kraal, his soldiers were lined up spick and span to greet him, raising their pith-helmets in a lusty cheer, while the smoke of the burning huts seemed almost to have dissipated already, and the savages looked on with repentant awe.

Pathos was permissible, even tragedy, but disorder or discomposure never, unless among the enemy. No imperial artist ventured to paint the Highlanders stumbling in panic from the summit of Majuba Hill, where in 1881 the Boers killed, wounded or captured 280 Britons for the loss of one burgher killed and five wounded, and if pictures did sometimes show rebels of the Indian Mutiny fastened for execution to the muzzles of guns, they were never actually being blown to bits. Self-control was everything, in this view of the imperial attitudes, and it was not surprising that easily the most successful of the imperialist artists was Elizabeth Butler, whose pictures were rich in heroic sacrifice, but meticulous in military detail – the right number of buttons on the soldier's jerkin, the correct bolt-action on the Martini-Enfield, above all the authentic cool discipline of the British Army, which surely never ran away, and certainly never lost its temper.

Sculptors, too, preferred the stately to the swashbuckling, and concentrated on viceroys, judges, generals, bas-reliefs of grateful natives and symbolic effigies of imperial types and virtues – pioneer farmers sowing corn in prairies, engineers consulting marble plans, soldiers on guard, explorers almost dead, scholars at whose feet grateful natives clustered. Triumphal statuary in the French manner (guns, rearing horses, battle standards waving) was not to the British imperial taste: a relatively effortless supremacy was the desired effect.

Most of all the sculptors sculpted Queen Victoria, and it was her ubiquitous effigy, carved by a thousand hands, erected in a thousand assorted sites, that must stand as the supreme imperial art form in the end. No great city of the Empire escaped its Queen Victoria – the royal statue was almost as essential to civic self-respect as figures of equestrian Romans had been in antiquity, or Henry Moore bronzes would be half a century later. The most satisfying of them, perhaps, were in hot parts of the Empire, for there the patina of equatorial lichens and insect-droppings, allied to the relentless rot of heat and damp, often combined to give the royal image a spurious sense of extreme age, and made it seem almost geologically part of the scene.

In Bombay the Queen-Empress sat beneath an immense canopy of carved marble, encrusted all over with medallions and jewelled embellishments at one of the principal intersections of the city centre: wrought iron railings protected her, and as the traffic rattled by on either side groups of Indians were generally to be seen bemusedly gazing at her across the gravel, as though she were stuffed. In Accra her bust was placed upon a tall stone column, and looked more sacramental: one approached it up a flight of steps, and bodyless as the figure was, and poised top-heavy there upon its pillar, it looked rather like some sacred reliquary, containing royal dust perhaps, or thigh-bones.

In Colombo Victoria sat high and magnificent upon a throne, well-busted and firmly-stayed, with pots of plants arranged gratefully around her as around a concert platform. And in Aden one saw her only dimly, through the blistering heat: for there she was deposited amidst a garden of thick vegetation, and while the shrubberies grew up around her feet, around her head the branches of palms depended: so that she seemed to be some half-secret presence there, to be approached only by initiates or municipal gardeners, and perhaps one day to be absorbed herself into the unity of nature, embraced at last within that native foliage, seduced by sinuous creeper.

At home in London the imperial art offered no such hints of mortality. The Empire seemed nothing if not muscular and alive, sexy even, with its swagger and its opulence, its tear-jerker tales and its heart-warming depictions. Its pressures were unremitting, and all the gifts of the great capital were applied to its glorification. If you bought a newspaper or a magazine it was sure to be full of empire: even *The Times* had succumbed to the craze, while the popular dailies blazoned the imperial glories in fervid headlines and columns of impassioned prose – the *Daily Mail* celebrated Queen Victoria's Diamond Jubilee with a special edition printed all in gold. Advertisers too enthusiastically exploited the theme – SOLDIERS OF THE QUEEN KNOW THE VALUE OF BOVRIL – BRITISH PLUCK TOBACCO BEATS ALL RIVALS –

> Naught shall make us Rue,
> If England to itself do rest but True,
> AND TAKES BEECHAM'S PILLS.

If you went to a concert you were likely to be bombarded with Elgar's *Pomp and Circumstance* marches, magnificent idealizations of militarism, especially when set to A. C. Benson's rousing words:

> *God who made Thee mighty*
> *Make thee mightier yet!*

If you went to a music-hall (particularly of course the Empire, Leicester Square) you would almost certainly get one of the swinging patriotic ballads of the time, 'Sons of the Sea', 'That's How We Made Our Name', or most appositely of all 'Another Little Patch of Red', and your evening would very likely end with a spectacular *tableau vivant* of Empire – Britannia herself centre-stage, surrounded by subjects in turbans or trappers' furs, with kangaroos and elephants in attendance and lions couchant right and left. If you were lucky enough to get tickets for the annual Royal Naval and Military Tournament you would enjoy thrilling re-enactments of actual imperial actions, against Boers or Zulus or Afghans or Sudanese, set against papier-mâché reconstructions of kraals or frontier forts, and played with full gallop of cavalry and blank blast of artillery – 'the militant spirit of our Empire', as one Tournament programme justifiably claimed, 'translated into Flesh and Blood'.

It was an inflamed atmosphere, at once alarming, exciting and impressive to sensitive visitors from abroad. It was as though an entire nation had been indoctrinated, but in a slightly frivolous or hair-brained way – as though the terrific issues of war, peace and dominion had been taken over by actor-managers, allied perhaps with fundamentalist sectarians. Even the demands of the expansionists for more battleships were turned into popular jingles – *We want eight and we won't wait* – and when Lloyd George the Welshman seemed about to suggest, at a meeting in 1901, that the Empire had no right to wage war against the Boers of South Africa, the audience responded with such ferocity that he was obliged to leave by a side entrance, and make his escape disguised as a policeman – for all the world as though he had uttered a blasphemy, or insulted some beloved comedienne.

Men of Imperial Letters: top left, W. E. Henley (1849–1903); top right, Rider Haggard (1856–1925);
above, war correspondents in the Second Boer War (sitting at right, Rudyard Kipling, 1865–1936)

'Queen Victoria Presenting a Bible in the Audience Chamber at Windsor'
T. Jones Barker, 1861

'Eastward Ho' Henry Nelson O'Neil, 1861

'Home Again' Henry Nelson O'Neil, 1859

'The Relief of Lucknow (Jessie's Dream)' Frederick Goodall, 1858

'Isandhlwana 1879': a print after a painting by Alfonse de Neuville of a
patrol of 17th Lancers discovering the bodies of two officers

'The Remnants of an Army' Lady Butler, 1879

'Last Indian Council Held on Canadian Soil Between the Governor-General (The Marquis of Lorne) and Crowfoot, Chief of the Blackfoot Indians 1881' Sydney Prior Hall

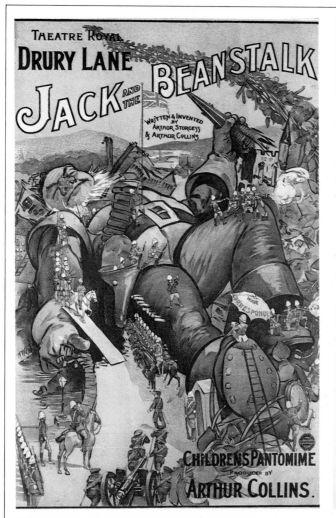

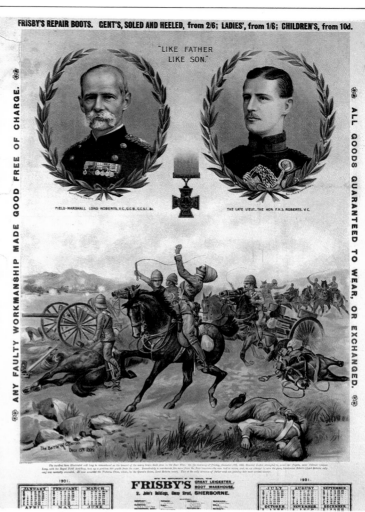

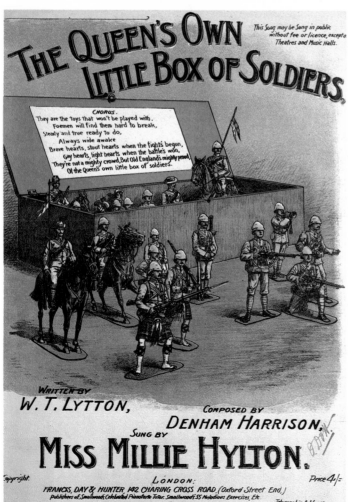

In the South African
War

BOVRIL

gave Vigor to the
Fighter,

Strength to the Wounded,
and
Sustenance to the Enteric.

Bovril formed an important part of the
Emergency Rations, and was one of the
principal supplies of both Base and Field
Hospitals throughout the Campaign.

The testimonials to the strengthening and sustaining power of Bovril would fill a book. They have been repeatedly included in the Official Reports of the Royal Army Medical Corps. They have formed part of the thrilling accounts of the newspaper correspondents. They have been embodied in the stories of eye-witnesses of scenes at the front and in the hospital tents. They have been part and parcel of the interesting letters written by the soldiers themselves to their relatives and friends at home. Doctors and nurses, officers and privates, soldiers and civilians, have pronounced the unanimous verdict that as a stimulating, nourishing, and sustaining food in the smallest compass, Bovril is without a peer.

Whether to the soldiers fighting at the front, or to the man at home battling against the inclemencies of the weather, weakness, and disease,

IS LIQUID LIFE.

Imperial advertising and propaganda, *c.* 1899

CHAPTER EIGHT

LIFE-STYLES

A Little Excursion, India, *c.* 1875

I t was not just in public performance that the British undertook their imperial duties in a stylized way. In private too, throughout their dominions, they tended to match their own self-image, and behaved in a manner which, while it might have begun as politic affectation, had become so ingrained that by the end of the nineteenth century it was perfectly natural.

It was not always their way at home in Britain. The imperial activists came chiefly from the middle classes, and were imbued in youth with all those particular inhibitions that came from the public schools, the Church of England, the proprieties of tennis court or cricket field. They were modest people by and large, diffident often, brought up to restraint and courtesy. But the moment they stepped on to dependent territories, they changed, involuntarily no doubt as a general rule, but sometimes quite consciously. They became, in a psychological sense, imperialists. In the white colonies they either adopted the louche irreverent attitudes of pioneers, or became more adamantly British than ever. In the African and Asian possessions they were promoted instantly into aristocrats, deferred to as they were by every indigene, obeyed by servants innumerable, finding themselves very likely to be administering territories as big as counties at home, or delegated powers of life and death when hardly out of their teens.

They acquired a miasma. Whatever their origins, whatever their jobs, they began to look alike. The army officer might have nothing to do with the jute merchant, the civil servant despise the railway engineer, but still to the outsider they were all members of a single elite, ready to close ranks at the first sign of external impudence. Kipling, travelling east from India for the first time in his life, was disconcerted by this unmistakable air of caste: at a party in Singapore he found everyone so familiar, the fat colonel, the flirtatious memsahib, the spinster fresh from home, that 'but for the little fact that they were entire strangers to me, I would have saluted them all as old friends'. And G. W. Steevens, on his way east in 1897, described his travelling companions thus: 'Fair haired, blue-eyed, square-shouldered and square-jawed, with puckered brows and steadfast eyes that seemed to look inwards and outwards at the same time, they were unmistakable builders – British empire builders.'

Everyone recognized this separateness, composed as it was partly of shyness, partly of arrogance, partly of defensive fraternity – the British well realizing that though they might be respected in the world of the Pax Britannica, they were seldom loved. If it was a comfort to the imperialists themselves, making them feel at once more authoritative and more secure, it was decisive too in keeping the natives in a proper condition. Britishness was Authority: the style *was* the Empire.

It was taken to allegorical extremes in the institution of the Club, a subtly potent factor in the British imperial system. The gentleman's club, its membership strictly limited, had been exported from London to every part of the Empire, and in cities like Sydney, Toronto or Cape Town had flowered into societies almost as grand, and just as rich, as its originals in Pall Mall and St James's. But as a means of political as against social dominance it found more obvious meaning in the Asian and African possessions of the Crown: for there it was developed as an enclave of power and privilege in an alien setting, its members patently different from the un-admitted millions not only in colour and status, but also in race.

Some such clubs were very impressive, like the Colombo Club in Ceylon for instance, an elegant oval-shaped structure above the sea, or the Madras Club, which was regally collonnaded and boasted the longest bar in India, or the Bengal Club which had expanded over the generations to include several town houses, and was almost like a little village of its own, or a royal compound. Some on the other hand were shabby up-country affairs of peeling shutters and corrugated iron, somnolent at noonday in the shattering heat, when only the languid waiters loitered around their empty rooms, boisterous in the evening when the Britons cast off their public images for an hour or two and reverted to island form.

Wherever they were, though, whatever their pretensions, the clubs of Empire had this in common: that they made the Right People feel more important, and made the Wrong People feel small. Let us test these effects for ourselves. We will choose a middle-rank club anywhere in the British tropics – a long low building with a verandah around it, and a weathervane of fish, fox or windjammer on top. Shingled red roof perhaps – windows shuttered against the fauna – dormers as a touch of Home – a gravel drive, sweeping past the watchman's box beside the gate to deposit carriages beneath its *porte-cochère*.

Outside, beside a fairly dessicated lawn of buffalo-grass, there are rows of potted geraniums: inside the main door, in the cool of teak and white paint, there are mingled smells of furniture polish, over-cooked vegetables, cigars and whisky – all delectably over-laid, if the place and the season are right, by the scent of the wood fire burning in the hall. A porter in a cubby-hole stares at us as we enter. An elderly military man, smoking a cheroot, inspects us steadily over the top of his newspaper. We pause self-consciously to examine the flutter of announcements on the notice-board – church services, hunt meets, bridge fixtures: then, 'Afternoon', says the Club Secretary, emerging suddenly from nowhere and approaching us with a steely smile, 'can I help you?'

If we are the right sort, all is well at once. We present our introductions, we sign the book, we are shown around the place, we are introduced to the military man in the hall, who claims to have thought he recognized us from the start. Soon we have a Scotch in our hands, and are surrounded by comfortable knick-knacks of our class and kind, like stuffed trout, framed cricket scores or the remarkable cravat habitually worn by A. S. Mortimer of Penang. *The Times* is there, not more than a few weeks old. So is *The Field*, and the Army List, and Ivey's Club Directory. The waiter takes our order as though he has known us all our lives. 'Harry!' comes a voice from the door. 'Heavens, my dear chap, how splendid to see you! Donald, you remember Harry Gribble don't you, lower Sixth the year before us? Bless my soul, it's like old times . . .'

But if we are Malay, Chinese, Zulu, Indian, by now we shall be feeling very different. We may speak the language perfectly, we may even have been in the lower Sixth ourselves, but we shall know that this sanctuary can never be for us. It is the enclave of a culture utterly self-sufficient and self-perpetuating, speaking dialects all its own, obeying nuances of behaviour and relationships that we can never understand. And anyway, even supposing that we had managed to get past the watchman at the gate, and the porter in that cubby-hole, the Secretary would never have let us further than the notice-board.

At the club the imperial Briton was likely to be living rather above himself, for its comforts were modelled upon those enjoyed by the greater landed gentry in England. In his own bungalow beneath the deodars, villa on the foreshore or clapboard house among the pines life was likely to be more modest in tone, but hardly less absolutely British. Generally speaking the imperialists, wherever they served, did their best to make their houses just like home. The dust storms might rage outside, the cruel winter winds rage off the prairie, the tropical rain, or the monkeys' feet, beat on the corrugated iron roof above: in the drawing-room things were likely to be much as they would be in Leatherhead or Chipping Camden.

Of course the furniture was mostly locally made, and was sometimes no more than a genial bazaar approximation of Chesterfield or Queen Anne. There might be straw matting on the floor, or tribal rugs instead of Mother's dear old Axminsters. There might be Tibetan trinkets here and there, a bit of Cree painting perhaps, a Zulu shield upon a wall, an elephant's foot. Mostly, though, the décor was likely to be faithfully British – the antimacassars, the Oxford frames, the upright piano, the trophies of sport, the fringed damask curtains, the potted plants, the samplers done by Aunt Mary in her childhood, the portraits of family, cricket XI or amateur dramatic society, the heavy brass lamps, the plethora of occasional tables, the careful assemblies of bric-à-brac on what-nots, the wedding cruets, the silver crumb-pan on the sideboard, the sofa-arm ash-trays shaped like saddles, with little spurs hanging below – all just as it would have been, just the same, if they had stayed at home in the first place.

There were exceptions naturally, for the Empire was never without non-conformists who preferred native life-styles to their own, and arranged their house altogether Fiji-style or *à l'Africaine*. The vast majority, though, stuck to what they knew best, reasoning that they were not out there to learn from the primitives, but to teach them proper values: and anyway, what had been good enough for Mother at the Rectory was certainly good enough for them in the Nazipur cantonment.

The British imperialists enjoyed themselves, as they conducted themselves, in ways peculiarly their own. Wherever the Empire implanted itself, almost immediately British kinds of pleasure burst into activity, and thus became official pleasures, so to speak. For the most part they were hardy outdoor pursuits, proper to an adventurous people, and for once the British did not keep their customs to themselves, but breezily shared them with the less debilitated of their subjects.

One of the happiest of the Empire's gifts to the world, indeed, undisputed even by its most unappeasable critics, was the gift of organized sport. It caught on almost everywhere. Peoples entirely unacquainted with the idea of the team spirit were initiated into all the mysteries of the English playing field, often taking to them with startling gusto – the Papuans played cricket with fifty-nine players a side, the Fijians compensated themselves for the end of cannibalism by taking up rugby football. Cricket in particular was encouraged, as a sort of epitome of the imperial values, and so the sounds, smells and ritual cries of the English national game became a familiar part of the imperial spectacle, the cry of *Howzat* ringing out from pitches of rolled gravel or stamped sand, and *There's a breathless hush in the Close tonight –*

> *A bumping pitch and a blinding light,*
> *An hour to play and the last man in*

– being recited at school prize-givings wherever the flag flew.

Everywhere the British settled, too, they threw themselves into blood sports. Any blood would do. Wherever a wild beast moved, wherever a fish jumped, wherever a game bird flew, the British were there to kill it – stuff it too, if possible, turn its skin into a hearth-rug, or mount its head heraldically in the hall. They hunted gazelle, hyena, wild pig, wolf, rhinoceros. In Australia, when hunting aborigines went out of fashion, they hunted kangaroo. In the Nilgiri Hills of India they met in meticulous hunting pink, attended by elegant whippers-in and well-bred packs of fox-hounds, to hunt the slinking jackal. Elsewhere they put together bobbery-packs of any old dog to hunt any old animal that came their way. The tiger-hunts of India were imperial occasions *in excelsis*, especially if there was a Viceroy or a visiting swell present: for then all was perfectly arranged, teams of elephants trundled docile through the bush, thousands of beaters drove the game the right way, hundreds of wild beasts were assured, and the subsequent group photograph showed the flushed sportsmen surrounded by heaps of dead *leo tigris*, teeth still bared in impotent defiance – a very figure of order over savagery, or Britain and the Beast.

Horse-racing was an addiction which always coloured the effect of Empire. The racecourse was as inescapable a feature of the British imperial settlement as the amphitheatre in a Roman town, or the bullring in Spain. Almost the moment the British arrived upon the scene – any scene – they improvised a race meeting. At Lhasa, when Younghusband led his mission to the abasement of the Dalai Lama, they raced around a dirt track with wild Tibetan ponies, the judge's stand being made of poles and rope, but a totalizer operating. At the other extreme the Melbourne Cup was one of the classiest occasions of the Australian year, bringing out imported hats and metropolitan accents in almost everyone, while on the day of the Viceroy's Cup at Calcutta, wrote an observer in the 1880s, 'the grandstand is filled with noble dames from England, from America and all parts of the world . . . In the paddock is a noble duke, a few lords, one or two millionaires from America and some serious politicians, who had visited this land to study the Opium Question.'

There were rich and unimpeachable racecourses; there were also impecunious and shady ones. At the Darjeeling track, which was claimed to be the smallest in the world, space was so limited that the racing ponies, when they had completed the circuit, were obliged to dash headlong off the course altogether, and down a neighbouring lane. And at the second race meeting ever held at Salisbury, Rhodesia, when the colony had been established for less than a year, Lord Randolph Churchill felt that his own horse, unexpectedly beaten by Dr Rutherfoord Harris's 'pig-fat cob', had almost certainly been nobbled.

If one had to reduce to a single impression the recreation of the imperial Establishment, one could best choose the hill station, the most distinctive urban innovation of the British Empire, and perhaps its most useful contribution to the gaiety of nations. The hill station was an Anglo-Indian device, but it spread to other parts of the Empire too, and wherever there was high ground above sweltering shore or arid flatland, the imperialists built themselves a cool retreat. Often Governors held summer court up there, giving the hill stations an air of worldly consequence for a few months every year: but they remained very small places, all of them, very intimate, nosy, intense places, whether they were intimate suburban retreats like the hill station of Penang Hill, which was only a couple of hours from the city streets of Georgetown, or Himalayan resorts like Simla, the summer capital of the entire Indian Empire, from where the Viceroy in his baronial mansion, attended by his army commanders, his foreign secretary, his financial advisers and his secret service, exerted the Queen's sway down the mountain slopes to plains and sea-ports far below.

The hill stations were usually on ridges, or at least on plateaus, affording the imperialists not only security against attack, but healthful breezes and fine views. They were mostly built to a pattern. An esplanade ran the length of the little town, now and then widening into a small piazza. Along it were the shops and public buildings, the Post Office, the Photographers by Appointment, the confectioners, the Raffles Tea Shop, Monsieur Arnold the Hairdresser, the Assembly Rooms, the Lyceum Theatre, where the amateur dramatic society played Gilbert and Sullivan or *School for Scandal* to fortunately indulgent audiences. At each end of town were the villas and bungalows of the British, Verbenia Lodge or Lavender Cottage, with the Club conveniently to hand, while at a more aloof distance stood the Governor's residence and the small army cantonment, from whose barrack square, in the clear mountain mornings, the call of the reveille bugle sounded across the valley. Clustered on the slopes of the ridge, in layered shacks and tenements down the precipitous hillside, picturesquely teemed the native quarters, lit by flickering woodfires at night, aromatic with smoke, incense, sweat and curry-powder.

The air was sparkling, there were prospects of snow-peaks above or dense jungle below, and upon this cramped and lively belvedere the imperial life-style took a curious turn. The imperialists lost a little of their imperialness up there. They wore their responsibilities less gravely. Incorruptible administrators held hands with grass widows, martinet colonels horseplayed, waves of gossip flowed in and around the villas and broke on tea-shop tables. In the hill stations the Empire actually came to seem an agency of pleasure: picnics in the woods, races at the jolly little racetrack, *HMS Pinafore* at the Lyceum (who would have thought Sir Oswald of the Finance Department could let his hair down so?), dances at the Assembly Rooms, long discursive teas, dressing up for the annual garden party at His Excellency's or just rollicking arm in arm in the crisp moonlight evenings down the Mall! It made you feel quite young again, as you did when you first came out, and you could almost forget the sad burdens of Empire (long hot slog in courthouse or office, lonely hours with nobody to talk to) that were awaiting you at the end of the season remorselessly down the rack railway below.

Such were the institutional life-styles of Empire. But there were unofficial life-styles too, and these were often very different. The Empire was a subjector of the coloured peoples, but it could be a liberator for the British themselves; for every imperialist who felt the urge to rule somebody else, there was an Empire-builder who disliked being ruled himself, and who found in the Victorian Empire a means of emancipation from authority, orthodoxy, bureaucracy, fuddy-duddy morality or parental interference.

Think what the Empire could do for a fellow! It could take him gold-hunting in the Yukon, where the whores of Dawson City cheerfully awaited his custom, the melodies of Snake Hips Lulu and the bar-room piano rung out brassily over snowy Saturday nights, and there was at least the off-chance of making a fortune. It could take him to the bridge of a paddle-steamer chugging high up the Murray river, where the gum trees stood silent over the muddy waters, where if he wasn't careful the beer fizzed in the heat of the sun, where wallabies and aboriginals flitted away at his passing like shadows through the scrub. It could give him a flock of sheep in the far-away Falklands, where no patronizing landlord would ever bother him again, and he could build his own square stone house just as he liked it in the lee of the moors.

It could make him a planter in Ceylon, looking out from his verandah over the smiling hills where the girls in their bright saris gracefully plucked his profits in the sunshine. It could appoint him a Hooghly river pilot, and send him out immensely posh, in white gloves and a gold-embroidered cap, to guide the steamships through the heat-glazed flats up-river to Calcutta. It could make him a newspaper editor in Hong Kong, or an Anglican dean in Belize, or a mountain guide in New Zealand, or a dentist in Malta, or a financial adviser to the Sultan of Johore, or a tutor to the children of the Maharajah of Mysore, or an inspector of light-houses in the Persian Gulf, or a dam-builder in Nubia, or the keeper of a botanical garden in Jamaica, or an elephant trainer in Burma, or a Fijian magistrate, or a New South Wales jockey, or an engine-driver on the Canadian Pacific, or a photographer in Durban, or a draper in Singapore, or one of the Shakespearian actors, the Shakespeare-wallahs, who from time to time turned up with their wandering troupes in the paint-peeled up-country halls of India.

Or it could make of him, very frequently, and happiest of all perhaps, one of the myriad bums of Empire, the loafers and beachcombers and itinerant philosophers, who roamed all the imperial frontiers, frequented every island strand, and turned up to shame the imperial hierarchy from Penang to Nootka Sound.

Life-styles: above, the Bengal Club, Calcutta; above right, servants at Mr Fletcher's house, Durban, Natal, 1894; right, The Sundowner, Gold Coast, *c.* 1890

Two views of Simla, the summer capital of the
Indian Empire, *c.* 1900

Little Imperialists: top, in Port Elizabeth, Cape Province, 1894;
above, in Tasmania, *c.* 1890; right, in Vancouver, British Columbia, 1901

Imperial Sports and Sportsmen: above, cricket at Simla, 1865 (the Sunday Picnic
Club XI *versus* the World); right, The Poona Crew, *c.* 1880

Imperial Sports and Sportsmen: left, tennis at Government
House, Grenada, 1896; above: The Chummery, *c.* 1880

The Hunt, Somewhere in India, *c.* 1900

The Poona Races, India, 1899

An Indian polo team plays for the Prince of Wales, *c.* 1876

Hunting scenes in Canada, *c.* 1900

Skinning the Tiger, India, *c.* 1880

35

The White Hunters: East African safaris, 1890s

Life-styles: imperialists of *fin-de-siècle* are seen (clockwise) awaiting the report of a game observer on top of a pole in East Africa; snipe-shooting and duck-hunting in India; driving a zebra-team, with mule at the rear, somewhere in South Africa

Pleasures of Egypt, 1907: above, A Fine Catch, Nile perch from Lake Qarun;
right, clockwise, the Cooks' steamer *Prince Abbas* at Abu Simbel; Lunch in the Tomb, Thebes;
a visit to the Valley of the Kings

In the Picnic Grounds: holiday time at north Vancouver, British Columbia, *c.* 1900

'Kangaroo Hunt' George French Anges, 1846

'Picnic Party at Hanging Rock near Mount Macedon' William Ford, 1875

'Self Portrait' Lt Frank Baden-Powell, 1885
Opposite, clockwise, 'Irish Emigrants' Erskine Nicol, 1864,
'The Prospector' Julian Ashton, 1889,
'Colonial Experience' J. A. Turner, *c.* 1899

'Civilian and His Wife Entertaining Officers to Dinner' anon, 1860

'A European Bungalow in Ceylon' Andrew Nicholl, _c._ 1847

On Stage: amateur dramatics at Darjeeling, India, 1872

Spreading the Word, 1890s: above, visiting the Kaffir Location, Port Elizabeth, Cape Province;
right, clockwise, the cathedral bells at Pietermaritzburg, Natal; Miss J. Thackeray
with young Christians, East Africa; Mrs Stone giving sugar to the natives of Zululand

Spreading the Word, 1890s: left, West Coast Indians pose
outside their church at Sechelt, British Columbia, and at St Mary's Mission,
not far away, fellow-Christians perform a Passion Play

Gold Rush: while miners of the Mucho Oro mine at Barkerville, British Columbia,
face the camera outside their mine-shaft, a consignment of new gold leaves Roxburgh, Central Otago,
under police escort in the 1880s, and Yukon prospectors take time off in their mess

The Sheep Farmers: mustering the flocks in New Zealand, 1900 (left);
shearing at Burrawarg, Australia (top);
the house in the clearing, New Zealand, 1900 (above)

On a Trinidad Cocoa Farm, 1893

In the Kimberley Diamond Mines: top, the Kaffir compound, 1894;
above, the hoisting-gears, 1875

OVERLANDERS (A
(MORNING COFFEE.)

Roughing It: The Pioneer's Wife, Australia; The Overlanders' Camp, Australia;
The Commercial Traveller, South Africa

EPILOGUE

The Funeral of Queen Victoria, London, 1901

The High Imperial effect did not last long. It depended upon the mood of supreme confidence which seized the British in the last quarter of the nineteenth century, and which made them feel, for a generation or two, that they could do anything – 'What other worlds have we to conquer?' as the Welsh-born Prime Minister of Australia, 'Billy' Hughes, once exuberantly cried. 'We are like so many Alexanders.' The humiliations of the Boer War shook this superbia, bringing the more imaginative British cruelly down to earth, and making a few of them even question the rightness of empire at all. In the middle of that conflict, before the imperial armies had achieved their inevitable final victory, Queen Victoria died: and with her went the virtue of the great adventure.

The Empire lingered on for another half century. Gradually, though, it lost the flare of its assurance, and became rather a parody of itself; its old disciplines were scorned now, its conventions were made to look absurd, and the grand idea itself, which had seemed so permanent, and which had worked so profitably, weakened and lost its nerve. Before long the Empire was ruled by men who did not believe in its future. Wars sapped its power, new perceptions weakened its convictions, and so, as the old shibboleths were discarded one by one, the imperial dogmas discredited, Queen Victoria's empire came to an end – leaving behind it, as the Cheshire cat left its enigmatic smile, the images that are recorded in this book.

Of course it was time it went, for it had outlived its functions and its opportunities, and of course there was much that was unforgivable to its passage across the continents. Yet there is a nagging excitement to its memory. A sense of waste is what one chiefly feels when one wanders among the imperial tombstones, rotted and fretted often now, darkened with lichen, toppled by neglect in their cemeteries around the world: but we can still experience something of the old challenge, still feel the thrill of the thing, by looking at its pictures.

There they all are still, gazing back at us from their gallery of the past. There are the sailors of a light cruiser, say, nonchalantly lolling around the ship's deck for their paying-off photograph, as merry a crew as ever you saw, some with their hats on the backs of their heads, some with their arms around each other's shoulders, laughing and smoking their pipes in the sunshine. There are the officers of some Indian cavalry squadron, Englishmen half-Indianified, part familiar, part very strange, swathed all about with weaponry, with sneering moustaches and turbans rakish on their heads. There is the memsahib on her verandah, all in white muslin. There is the bishop sun-tanned in his canonicals. The Most Superior Person rides by in a howdah. The War-Lord points a finger at us. Radiantly Younghusband looks down the years from his hilltop outside Lhasa.

An Australian grazier takes a drink upon his lonely homestead porch – 'Cheers, sport!' Half a dozen speculators sit in an aura of wealth outside the Kimberley Club, holding glasses and big cigars. An amateur dramatic society poses elaborately costumed and much too warm for comfort, during an intermission in the dress rehearsal somewhere very hot. Snake Hips Lulu and other ladies of Klondyke pleasure smile at us in the cold sun during an off-duty frolic. Here come the victors of Ashanti, bronzed and pleased, greeted with flowers, kisses and brass bands as they file down the troopship gangplank. There go the soldiers of the Second Boer War, rifles slung across their shoulders, still whistling 'Goodbye Dolly Grey' as they march on to another Spion Kop, perhaps, the murderous fire of another Magersfontein, or battles far more terrible still beyond the frame of the imperial effect.

Gone, all gone, their very world disintegrated: only their images remain to haunt us, and make us wonder still.

Trefan Morys, 1982

Archie Chamberlin's Bungalow, Ceylon

Young Official on Camel-back, Lahore

Imperial Interior, East Africa

A Missionary Bishop in the Field

A Hunting Trip in Kashmir

At the End of the March: men of the King's Royal Rifle Corps, South Africa, 1901

THE BRITISH EMPIRE,1900

Population *c* 400m

Area 11,288,000 square miles

Imports £809,178,200 ($3,884,041,360)

Exports £658m ($3,158,400,000)

Total trade £1,467,178,200 ($7,042,441,360)

Territories

In Europe: Great Britain and Ireland: Channel Islands: Gibraltar: Isle of Man: Malta

In America: Bahamas: Barbados: British Guiana: British Honduras: British Virgin Islands: Canada: Falkland Islands: Jamaica: Leeward Islands: Newfoundland: Tobago: Trinidad: Turks and Caicos Islands: Windward Islands

In Asia: Aden: Brunei: Ceylon: Hong Kong: India: Labuan: Malay Federated States: North Borneo: Papua: Sarawak: Straits Settlements

In Africa: Ashanti: Basutoland: Bechuanaland: British East Africa: Cape Province: Gambia: Gold Coast: Natal: Nigeria: Nyasaland: Orange Free State: Rhodesia: Sierra Leone: Somaliland: Transvaal: Uganda: Zanzibar

In Australasia: New South Wales: New Zealand: Queensland: South Australia: Tasmania: Victoria: Western Australia

In the Atlantic Ocean: Ascension: Bermuda: St Helena: Tristan da Cunha

In the Indian Ocean: Mauritius: Seychelles: seven other groups and islands

In the Pacific Ocean: Ellice, Gilbert, Southern Solomon, Union archipelagos: Fiji: Pitcairn: twenty-four other groups, islands and reefs.

Egypt and the Sudan were under British military occupation. Cyprus was British-administered, but nominally under Turkish sovereignty.

Administration The India Office and the Colonial Office both had their offices in Whitehall, London, and each was represented in Parliament by a Secretary of State. The Crown was represented throughout the Empire by Viceroys, Governors-General, Governors, Residents, Administrators and High Commissioners. The foreign relations of the entire Empire were conducted by the Foreign Office in London. Self-governing colonies were represented in the imperial capital by Agents.

WHO WAS WHO IN 'LIVING LEGENDS'

Baden-Powell, Robert Stephenson Smyth, 1st Baron, 1857–1941: a national hero for his sprightly defence of Mafeking against the Boers in 1899–1900, while still a serving soldier he founded the Boy Scout movement, and retiring as a general in 1910 spent the next 30 years fostering its growth across the world.

Baring, Evelyn, 1st Earl Cromer, 1841–1917: 'Overbaring', professional soldier of a well-known banking family who became British Agent and Consul-General in Egypt – that is to say, *de facto* ruler of the country – from 1883 to

1907, evolving a system of control known delicately as 'The Veiled Protectorate'.

Curzon, George Nathaniel, 1st Marquess Curzon of Kedleston, 1859–1925: scholar, explorer and politician who became Viceroy of India in 1899, but was obliged to resign in 1905 because of differences with Lord Kitchener, the British commander-in-chief in India. He became Foreign Secretary and Chancellor of Oxford University, but died disappointed at his failure to become Prime Minister.

Fisher, John Arbuthnot, 1st Baron, 1841–1920: brilliant, pugnacious and controversial naval officer whose reforms as First Sea Lord between 1904 and 1910 transformed the nature of the Royal Navy. Recalled during the first world war, he fell from grace after the catastrophe of the Dardenelles, and went into fuming retirement in 1915.

Gordon, Charles George, 1833–1885: 'Chinese' Gordon, engineer officer who first became famous for his military exploits in the service of the Chinese Emperor, but achieved apotheosis when Gladstone sent him to Khartoum in 1884 to evacuate Egyptian forces from Khartoum in the Sudan, then threatened by the forces of the rebellious Mahdi. For reasons still uncertain he delayed withdrawal until too late, and was killed on the steps of his palace by the Nile in 1885.

Jameson, Sir Leander Starr, 1853–1917: colonial physician, who made his name as leader of the abortive Jameson Raid designed to overthrow Boer rule in Johannesburg in 1895, and who survived the disgrace of its fiasco to become Prime Minister of Cape Colony and a leading statesmen of the new Union of South Africa.

Kitchener, Horatio Herbert, 1st Earl, 1850–1916: engineer officer who came to prominence as commander-in-chief of the Egyptian Army in 1892. After victories over the Mahdi in the Sudan, and the Boers in South Africa, Kitchener emerged as the leading British soldier of his day, and became successively commander-in-chief in India, British Agent and Consul-General in Egypt, and finally Secretary of State for War, in which capacity he mobilized the British Army for the first world war. He was drowned while *en route* for an official mission in Russia.

Livingstone, David, 1813–1873: Scottish missionary and explorer whose immense African journeys made him world-famous: having discovered the Victoria Falls in 1855, in 1866 he began his great (but unsuccessful) expedition to identify the sources of the Nile, in the course of which he died.

Lugard, Frederick John Dealtry, 1st Baron, 1858–1945: professional soldier who, as Governor of Nigeria, became celebrated for his theories of indirect rule, expressed in his seminal book *Dual Mandate in British Tropical Africa*, 1922.

Milner, Alfred, 1st Viscount, 1854–1925: German by ancestry and early education, after brief excursions into academic life and journalism Milner joined the British administration in Egypt, and then as British High Commissioner in southern Africa played a crucial role in precipitating the Boer War of 1899, and in the settlement that followed, which he saw as an opportunity to establish permanent British supremacy. He was briefly Colonial Secretary after the first world war, but had really burnt himself out by then.

Rhodes, Cecil John, 1853–1902: financier and speculator who made a fortune in South African mines, and used it to extend British imperial influence – first by establishing the Colony of Rhodesia, then by founding Rhodes Scholarships at Oxford. He became Prime Minister of Cape Colony in 1890, but was forced to resign because of his implication in the ill-fated Jameson Raid, and died under a cloud, though rich as ever.

Younghusband, Sir Francis Edward, 1863–1942: after some brilliant explorations in Central Asia, represented the British Indian Government in a mission to Lhasa in 1903, but was converted by the experience to peaceful and mystical pursuits, becoming President of the Royal Geographical Society and publishing numbers of books like *Within* (1912) and *Life in the Stars* (1927), besides founding the World Congress of Faiths in 1936.

INDEX

ACKNOWLEDGEMENTS

The author and publishers wish to thank the following for permission to reproduce photographs:

Alexander Turnbull Collection, Wellington, New Zealand, pages 22 below, 104, 238 above, 240 and 241 below right; Art Gallery of New South Wales, pages 132 and 230 above right; Australian Consolidated Press, pages 241 above right, 244 above and 244 below; BBC Hulton Picture Library, pages 33 below, 34 above, 34 below, 70, 79, 82 above, 84, 85, 86, 87 above, 88, 90 left, 92, 101, 114 above, 164, 188, 197, 218, 222, 223 right, 224 above, 246 and 248 above right; Birmingham Reference Library, pages 37 right, 38, 51 right, 52, 59 below right, 62, 63, 64, 65, 67, 128, 207 above, 210 above, 226, 227, 234, 235 above left, 235 below, 242, 243 and 245; Bridgeman Art Library, pages 25 above, 53 above, 53 below, 130/131, 162, 180 above and 229 above; Mrs A. C. Cowell, pages 28 above and 129 above; Eyre and Hobhouse Art Gallery, pages 129 below and 232 below; Thomas Gilcrease Institute of American History and Art, Tulsa, Oklahoma, pages 194/195; Glenbow-Alberta Institute, pages 158, 169 and 220 above; Gordon Boy's School, page 72; Kenneth Griffith, pages 82 below and 196; Bernard Higton, pages 150/151; John Hillelson Agency, pages 33 above, 60/61, 99, 137, 159 right, 160, 198 and 224/225; India Office Library, pages 10, 21, 22 above left, 22 above right, 23, 31, 35, 39, 87 below, 105, 108, 143, 163, 165 below and 232 above; Kodak Museum, pages 166 and 167; Kevin MacDonnell, pages 57, 89, 91, 146, 172, 173 right, 174, 176 left, 177, 178 and 181; Mansell Collection, pages 19, 20, 32, 100, 182; National Army Museum, London, pages 24 above, 145 above, 149 below, 157, 165 above, 180 below, 191 and 231; National Gallery of Canada, Ottawa, pages 68/69; National Gallery of Victoria, Melbourne, pages 54 above left and 229 below; National Library of Ireland, page 144; National Maritime Museum, London, pages 50 and 161 above; National Portrait Gallery, pages 71, 80/81 and 189; New South Wales Government Printing Office, Australia, pages 8/9, 123 and 175; Popperfoto, pages 34 centre, 40, 49 above, 55, 110, 111 below, 114 below, 115, 142 above, 208/209 and 212; Public Archives of Canada, pages 112 left and 113; Royal Commonwealth Society, pages 16 left, 17, 36, 102, 109 above right, 111 above, 122 above left, 125, 127, 134, 135, 136, 142, 206 and 214; Royal Geographical Society, pages 29, 30, 59 above right, 66 above, 106, 107, 124, 126 left, 207 below, 213, 215, 216/217, 221, 225 above left, 225 above right and 233; Royal Photographic Society, pages 49 below, 219 and 249 above; Sean Sexton, page 168; Sheffield City Art Gallery, pages 190 below and 230 above left; Sotheby Parke Bernet, pages 54 above right, 179 and 230 below; State Library of Tasmania, pages 56 left, 103 right, 109 below right, 133, 145 below, 171 right and 210 below; Tate Gallery, London, page 192/193; Telecom Australia, South Australia, page 122 below left; United Society for the Propagation of the Gospel, pages 235 above right, 248 below left and 248 below right; Vancouver Public Library, pages 24 below, 58, 66 below, 116, 138, 139, 140, 141, 170, 211, 228, 236, 237 right, 238 below and 239; Walker Art Gallery, pages 149 above and 152; Christopher Wood Gallery, pages 190 above left and 190 above right. The pictures on pages 25 below, 26/27, 28 below, 54 below and 161 below are reproduced by gracious permission of Her Majesty the Queen.

The author and publishers also wish to thank The National Trust for permission to quote from 'Recessional' (on page 182) by Rudyard Kipling, and Peter Newbolt for permission to quote from 'Clifton Chapel' (on page 184) and 'Vitaï Lampada' (on page 202) by Henry Newbolt.